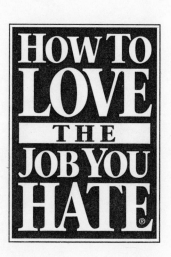

HOW TO
LOVE
THE
JOB YOU
HATE

Dear Allan,
I feel honored to
have you in my class
today. Follow His leading
and you will know what
to do cre. The work situation!
I am so proud
of you! Blessings,
Jane

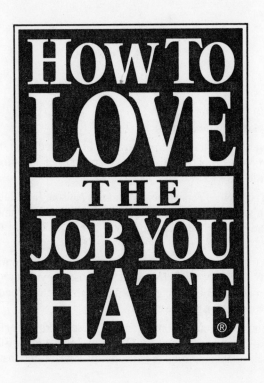

HOW TO LOVE THE JOB YOU HATE

Jane Boucher

THOMAS NELSON PUBLISHERS
Nashville

Published in Nashville, Tennessee, by Thomas Nelson, Inc., Publishers, and distributed in Canada by Word Communications, Ltd., Richmond, British Columbia, and in the United Kingdom by Word (UK), Ltd., Milton Keynes, England.

Unless otherwise noted, Scripture quotations are taken from the HOLY BIBLE, NEW INTERNATIONAL VERSION ®. Copyright © 1973, 1978, 1984 by International Bible Society. Used by permission of Zondervan Bible Publishing House. All rights reserved.

The "NIV" and "New International Version" trademarks are registered in the United States Patent and Trademark Office by International Bible Society. Use of either trademark requires the permission of International Bible Society.

Illustrator: Craig Schaefer.

Library of Congress Cataloging-in-Publication Data

Boucher, Jane.

  How to love the job you hate / Jane Boucher.

    p. cm.

  Includes bibliographical references.

  ISBN 0–8407–7819–8 (pbk.)

  1. Job satisfaction. 2. Self-esteem.   I. Title.

HF5549.5.J63B68   1994

650.1—dc20   93–37821

                                               CIP

Printed in the United States of America

1 2 3 4 5 6 7 — 00 99 98 97 96 95 94

Contents

Special Section for Employers

Conclusion

Acknowledgments

This book has been a dream come true. For many years, I have had a deep concern for American workers and their level of happiness on the job. We expend most of our energy during our workday, and our families get what's left of us. What happens to us at work affects every other area of our lives. It is my hope that as you read these words, you will find comfort and practical tools that will help you achieve greater peace on the job and at home.

I could not have written this book without inspiration, and it is to God that I give the credit.

But the ideas have to take form. Geoffrey R. Lorenz, president and CEO of the Lorenz Corporation, took my idea, believed in it, and transformed it into a reality. I thank you, Geoff, for walking the talk and for your belief in this project. Without you, I doubt this would have been possible.

Carl Lekic, general manager of the Harley Sandcastle, provided an environment at his lovely hotel on the Sarasota, Florida beach where I could write and be inspired.

For your creative input and research, Kathy Spoon and Carol Williams, and your art work, Craig Schaefer, I am deeply grateful. Any endeavor is greatly enhanced when several minds come together toward a common goal. You, too, helped make my dream become a reality.

And, Duncan Jaenicke, you have been a guiding light throughout the project. Thank you for your wisdom and insight.

Many others have been instrumental in the development of this project. I am deeply grateful to my clients who have allowed me to grow their organizations. Many of the stories in this book come from my experiences with them.

Every author needs emotional support, and mine has come largely from Tom Hawley, and my mentor, LaVina Wilson. She is a retired inner-city missionary and a willing, yielded vessel of God's power and love.

I thank my parents who taught me how to be a survivor. They encouraged me to get an education and to overcome any obstacle. They taught me to say, "I can do it!"

There is no way I could have written this book without the loving support and guidance from Dr. Judith Pistilli. Written words cannot describe my gratitude to her.

I couldn't possibly forget to mention my dearest feline friend, Mr. Bo Jangles, who sat lovingly in my lap while most of this book was being written.

My last acknowledgment goes to you, the reader, for without you, there would be no reason to write this book. I hope you enjoy reading it as much as I enjoyed writing it.

Foreword

The nation's most admired (and hated) CEO, Jack Welch of GE, believes in two of his keys to success: a positive winning attitude and self-confidence with a perpetual touch of reality.

How does one further learn the A, B, C's of those two and several other success factors? The best way is to follow a proven practitioner. Jane Boucher, whom I have watched and worked with through the last decade, is that professional.

As an operational head of Delco Moraine, I had a team of more than four thousand who produced billions of auto brakes that worked 100 percent of the time. Always! The unity of those folks, who at one time were adversarial and distrusting, was a core issue to my management challenge. Although we tapped into lots of help, Jane's was among the best. We created the most reliable brake team!

With numerous giants "right-sizing" today, those who must survive will profoundly benefit from Jane's work. If 90 percent of Americans do hate or even mildly dislike their jobs, there is bound to be further decay in our global competitiveness as well as in our families. Jane's "potentializing" works and, therefore, offers a sound, basic solution.

Her book is full of down-to-earth, how-to guidelines against the backdrop of profound, easy-to-relate-to philosophical imagery. It elevates the mind and trains it at the same time. Not many people can change on their own, and those who want to may need to select from a wide variety of panaceas. From a purely practical point of view, this work should rise to the top. Read it and share it with those you love and . . . with the others you hate. It will challenge you to change; the rest is in your control.

John Curley,
Retired Director of Operations,
General Motors/Delco

Preface

The title *How To Love The Job You Hate*® may sound a little harsh, but most of us do *hate* our jobs at some time or another. No matter how much you love what you do, the people you work with, or the challenges you face, there will always be days when you want to scream, "I hate this job!"

That is partly why I chose this title, but I also chose it because of the incredible rise in job dissatisfaction that is occurring all over the country.

This book is intended to be a how-to guide. That is why you will find numerous lists of specific actions to take on your job right now. Of course, I can't guarantee the results, but I can tell you that the lists were compiled from the real experiences of people, including myself, who have tried them and found them to work. My prayer is that they will work for you too.

Though most of the chapters are written to the reader as an employee, I have included a section that speaks directly to employers, or people who supervise others. However, everyone should read the entire book. It applies to everyone who works because employees and employers are all part of the same team. I believe the key to loving the job you hate is trust—trust flowing both ways between employee and employer.

I have used many anecdotal stories in the book to illustrate how the suggestions work. Though these are composite stories, taken from hundreds of my students all over the country and are not based on any one person, each story is based on real situations.

So try these practical suggestions. See if you can begin to turn TGIF (Thank God It's Friday) into TGIM (Thank God It's Monday). At the very least, I hope you won't dread Monday quite so much. You might even find yourself saying, "I love this job!"

The Lean-Mean Corporate Machine!

Why Do You Hate Your Job? The Work Force in Transition

1

Kenny, a thirty-year-old computer programmer, flies across the country two to three times a week to unravel the latest computer problems for his company's clients. At first, the travel was exciting to Kenny. He even goes to Hawaii a couple of times a year. But after three years of constant travel, as well as having moved his wife and small son three times in those three years to three different parts of the country, he's not as excited any more. He receives an excellent salary and incredible benefits, but he's overweight, gets no exercise, suffers from jet lag most of the time, rarely sees his wife, who must cope with the moves to new communities virtually alone, and fears becoming a stranger to his young son.

Kenny is beginning to suffer from the debilitating epidemic that has swept America in the last two decades: the "I hate my job" syndrome. If you are like Kenny, you may have a job, you may be making good or adequate money, and you may even love the work you're doing. But you may also feel stressed and trapped. You are not alone. Statistics vary, depending on who's taking the poll and when it was taken, but in the last few years numerous polls taken by *Business Week*, Gallup, and others have indicated that anywhere from 83 to 92 percent of the people in this country are not happy with their jobs. That is reflected in the fact that businesses lose more than $150 billion each year to absenteeism, lowered productivity, staggering medical insurance costs, and the rehiring and retraining of workers, according to the Cigna Corporation.

The Cigna Corporation also calculates that more than a million people call in sick every day in this country. If you've noticed that you suffer from colds and sinus infections, stomach problems, and various forms of back or neck pain more frequently, you are suffering from three of the most common stress-related ailments.

Or perhaps you experience symptoms that are more emotional than physical. You may not be a particularly peppy person in the morning, but do you find it especially difficult to get out of bed? Is your mind flooded with thoughts of work as you're getting ready? Do you find yourself prolonging the drive to the office, stopping for gas when you really don't need it or thinking up other errands you can perform as an excuse for being late?

Perhaps you're one of those chronically tardy people who can never manage to get to work on time no matter how many warnings you receive or how early you get up. Or, if you don't come in late, maybe you spend as much time as you can in the restroom or in someone else's office where you're not likely to be found for a while. Though you may not realize it, those are all symptoms of trying to avoid the inevitable—your job.

Perhaps you or someone you work with has fallen into the chronic complainer habit. Sometimes it's good to let off steam by telling someone you're close to about your rough day at work. That's normal even for people who are happy in their jobs. But it can get out of control if you are not careful to monitor yourself. Do you start every free moment or weekend talking about everything that went wrong at work and continue to complain until you go back to work on Monday? Did you enjoy your weekend? Of course not. Your unhappiness at work is ruining your happiness at home.

You may be the type who doesn't seem to exhibit emotional or health problems and appears relatively happy on the job. You're always joking and laughing, but as soon as you leave work you feel like a child being let out of school or an inmate being let out of prison. You head straight for your favorite "stress-reliever," which may be alcohol or drugs or nothing more than food or TV. Any of those things can become serious addictions when constantly used to help you forget your unhappy situation at work.

In the nineties there is another problem that makes the "I hate my job" syndrome even worse: guilt. How can you justify hating or even complaining about your job in light of the current situation in the economy? After all, a lot of people are losing their jobs these days. In late 1991 and early 1992, companies announced massive layoffs of both blue-collar and white-collar workers, and job cutting is continuing well into the mid-nineties.

General Motors announced plans to cut its North American work force by 74,000 and close 21 plants. Colgate-Palmolive announced plans to trim 2,000 workers from its worldwide work force. PepsiCo announced the elimination of 1,800 management and administrative jobs at its Frito-Lay unit. Time Warner said it will lay off 105 editorial workers. Mead corporate headquarters plans to cut 1,000 jobs from its nationwide work force. Even retail giant Sears announced the closing of more than 200 stores and catalog outlets and the discontinuation of its famous catalog, all costing about 50,000 jobs.

IBM, once America's most feared and respected company, announced its first mass layoff in history, attempting to reduce its work force by up to 25,000 jobs. Stock dividends at IBM were cut in an attempt to revive the declining company. Xerox, Kodak, TRW, Unisys, and many more of America's corporate elite are no longer havens of job security.

A slump in the airline industry has weakened the demand for jetliners, resulting in several thousand jobs being slashed at Boeing and Pratt & Whitney. Airlines are laying off—United announced plans to cut 40,000 jobs. Many airlines are going completely out of business or being bought out, including Piedmont, Braniff, Eastern, and Midway.

It all sounds pretty bleak, but that is why this book was written. There is a light at the end of the tunnel. There's hope for the country, the work force, and you. You can change things right where you are, in the very job you may hate right now. You'll find out how in the pages that follow.

Why Do Americans Hate Their Jobs?

Just what is causing all this economic upheaval and dissatisfaction? We're right in the middle of a new revolution.

The industrial revolution occurred between 1750 and 1850 mainly in Britain and spread to other countries during the mid to late 1800s. Machines, electricity, steam, and gasoline engines created the factory system for large-scale production. The laboring population, formerly employed mainly in agriculture, increasingly gathered in urban industrial centers. After the Civil War, industry became the dominant economic factor in American life.

Industry revolutionized our lifestyle, providing an economic base for population expansion and improvement in living standards. It also created many unforeseen problems such as labor and management conflicts and environmental pollution. You've probably heard stories from grandparents or read in history books about the sweatshops of the industrial revolution. Men, women, and children worked twelve to sixteen hours a day in hot, dirty factories under appallingly unsafe conditions. Despite these difficulties, wages rose fivefold, and the value of production rose sixfold between 1900 and 1920.[1]

This manufacturing economy continued unabated through World War II. After the war, other countries, such as Japan, benefited from American reconstruction assistance and began industrializing their economies as well. Japan, in fact, became so good at industrialization that it has surpassed the United States in many market areas, most notably electronics and automobiles.

In the early 1950s another revolution began: the "computer revolution." Computers became smaller and more sophisticated, leading to their application in increasing numbers of industries. Computers began changing the face of our work economy from blue-collar to "silicon-collar." Consequently, the United States' manufacturing economy began to decline because of increased foreign competition and rapidly changing technology. The industrial revolution took 100 to 150 years to fully complete its economic changes, but the computer has caused almost as much change in the last twenty to thirty years.

The United States' work force has gone from a manufacturing economy to a technical, service, and information economy. Companies forced into this transition fear that they can no longer afford to take care of employees for life. They are struggling to keep their business afloat. They are eliminating some types of work and expanding others. When downsizing and restructuring doesn't solve the problems, many companies are not able to survive, as is evidenced by numerous closings of smaller businesses, mergers, and buyouts, such as AT&T's takeover of NCR.

After the decline in the manufacturing economy, transitional survival efforts eliminated hundreds of thousands of manufacturing jobs during the eighties. But the trend continues to work its way up in the nineties and entire layers of middle management jobs are also being eliminated. According to the Bureau of Labor Statistics, about 10 percent of unemployed workers in 1991 were from managerial or professional backgrounds, up from 7.5 percent in previous years. Of 910 companies surveyed by the American Management Association, a record 55 percent laid off employees in the 12 months ending June 30, 1991. That was up from 36 percent in the previous 12 months. During that period, 71 percent of wholesale and retail trade employers, 60 percent of manufacturers, and 59 percent of business and professional service firms reported job cuts.

What was the main reason behind those layoffs? The American Management Association survey reports that 73 percent of firms said business was bad or was expected to get worse, up from 55 percent in 1990. Of course, with all those job losses, the consumer economy is also ailing. It's the proverbial Catch-22: industry is changing, so jobs are cut to regain profits; but when jobs are cut, business declines, so profits are lost and more jobs are cut.

The nineties will prove to be the decade when the American work force makes the final full shift into the information age. Who will be the survivors? Will America regain its top position in competitive global markets? Will an entire generation of unskilled workers add to the country's already intolerable number of homeless and welfare dependents?

It is imperative to keep in mind that all of these problems are symptoms of a transition. The United States is in the critical stages now, but history shows that we can survive the transition and create a new golden age, if we learn from past mistakes and remain open to the changes the future will bring. As the bestseller *Megatrends 2000* points out, we are moving into a global information economy, with change being driven by telecommunications and computers, just as manufacturing drove change in the industrial period.

Megatrends 2000 also tells us what our most valuable competitive edge is: "In the global economic boom of the 1990s, human resources are the competitive edge for both companies and countries . . . the quality and innovativeness of human resources will spell the difference."[2]

Right now, because economic insecurity is running high and many businesses are running scared, some desperate measures are being used as survival tactics. The trend in business is toward the "lean and mean." Fewer people are being asked to do more work in order to maintain profits. Public companies are working for short-term gains that keep stock prices up and corporate raiders away. That has caused more companies to encourage management to focus on the bottom line. The quality-oriented managers and executives with a strong commitment to employee pride and customer satisfaction are behind. Unfortunately, that has not been the best solution for America's workers or consumers. It has resulted in discontent affecting all occupations, job levels, types, and sizes of organizations across the country.

Consider some examples of bottom-line oriented management and its effects on workers:

- Telephone operators are monitored by computers. They are required to complete an answered call within a specified number of seconds as the computer keeps track. The purpose is to shave one second from every call the operator answers and save the company $1 million a year. The costs of this measure, including stress, employee turnover and absenteeism, wrong numbers and wrong information given out, were in fact much higher. A number of operators also developed carpal tunnel syndrome, a wrist injury often requiring surgery, as a result of working faster on their keyboards to keep up with the computer monitor.

- Salaried employees who are not eligible for overtime pay are assigned all overtime work in one small firm, so that no overtime has to be paid to hourly employees. The tactic saves money for the company but has resulted in overworked, resentful salaried employees and a high degree of turnover. If the manager who implemented the policy were to figure the cost of interviewing, rehiring, and retraining all the new employees the practice has generated, the savings would most likely turn into a substantial loss.

- Employees in one company are supposed to receive bonuses at the end of the year based on how much extra work and dedication they give during the year. During one particular year, a lot of extra work was done on proposals for new business. Because no profit was made on the proposal work itself and despite the fact that most of the proposals were successful, the company told employees that it could not afford to pay bonuses that year. Considering the

damage to morale, the company should have realized it
could not afford *not* to keep its promise and pay bonuses to
reward the extra efforts of its employees.

Fortunately, many businesses are beginning to realize that this
method of management is costing more in the long-term than it is
saving in the short term. They are recognizing that the only way to
survive in the nineties and beyond is to have workers who are happy
in their jobs and have a sense of loyalty to their companies. Managers
are learning the advantages of being sensitive to workers' personal
needs and motivations. In a sense they are learning the golden rule of
business: do unto your workers as you would have your workers do
unto the company.

What Can We Learn from Our Toughest Competitors?

Americans tend to believe that the Japanese are the best in the world
at running businesses and managing people. Yet, in a survey of
Japanese workers, only 17 percent reported that they were very satisfied with their jobs.[3] Other comparative surveys have shown that even
though economic conditions are worse in the United States than in
Japan, only 67 percent of Japanese people are satisfied with their
overall quality of life, whereas 81 percent of Americans are satisfied.[4]
The Japanese work the longest hours in the world: twelve hours a
day, six days a week, for a staggering seventy-two hour workweek.
Despite their nation's wealth, the prohibitive costs of food, housing,
and entertainment and the short supply of leisure time leave the
Japanese feeling personally unfulfilled. Job-related stress has resulted
in alcoholism, depression, suicide, and the destruction of families.
Many Japanese workers have even developed unique guilt- and stress-
related symptoms that leave them physically ill on weekends but
subside when it's time to go back to work on Monday. In fact, up to
10,000 Japanese die annually as victims of *karoshi*, or "death by
overwork."[5]
Japan is a nation that is out of balance. It has sacrificed personal
satisfaction and happiness to become one of the strongest economic
powers in the world. We can probably learn a lot from Japan about

production methods and quality control, but it is not a model of how to achieve greater satisfaction on the job.

What Do Americans Want from Their Jobs?

What is job satisfaction? A recent Gallup poll sheds some light on what is most important to Americans and how satisfied they are with the following aspects of their jobs.[6]

	Very Important	Completely Satisfied
Good health insurance and other benefits	81%	27%
Interesting work	78	41
Job security	78	35
Opportunity to learn new skills	68	31
Annual vacations of a week or more	66	35
Being able to work independently	64	42
Recognition from coworkers	62	24
Having a job in which you can help others	58	34
Limited job stress	58	18
Regular hours, no nights or weekends	58	40
High income	56	13
Working close to home	55	46
Work that is important to society	53	34
Chances for promotion	53	20
Contact with a lot of people	52	45

It is not surprising that health insurance, benefits, and job security are at the top of the list these days, but look how far down high income is listed. In all kinds of surveys done in the last several years, pay consistently ranks relatively low as an important component of job satisfaction. But number two, interesting work, consistently appears near the top, often in the number one slot. It has long been known that interesting work is one of the most important components of job satisfaction.

Looking at the rating of satisfaction in these areas, however, tells a sad story of how Americans feel about their jobs. None of the satisfaction ratings even reaches the halfway mark. In other words, more than one-half of those polled felt that the things most important to them about their jobs are far less than satisfactory. Only 41 percent say they do interesting work, yet 78 percent believe that is vitally important. Stress is another area that is highly unsatisfactory, with only 18 percent saying they experience limited stress. And though income was ranked fairly low in importance, there is a high rate of dissatisfaction in that area, with only 13 percent satisfied.

You Can Work toward Greater Job Satisfaction

This book has been written to help you in those areas of importance that you can personally work to change in your job. Though you may not have much control over your health insurance, benefits, or job security, you can have a definite and positive effect on:

- Making and keeping your work interesting
- Finding opportunities to learn new skills
- Being able to work independently
- Gaining recognition from coworkers
- Helping others in your job
- Limiting job stress and its effects
- Eliminating unnecessary overtime hours
- Seeing your work as important to society
- Enhancing your chances for promotion
- Increasing your contact with a lot of people

Actually, improving those areas does help make your job more secure in the current economic situation, because achieving greater satisfaction makes you a happier, more productive worker. In turn, you become a more valuable employee and less likely to be sacrificed when cuts are forthcoming. Learning to enhance your job satisfaction can even help you survive a job loss and make a smoother transition to a new position.

So, if the lean, mean corporate machine is getting you down, take heart! Even if your company isn't one of the more enlightened ones that is learning the golden rule of business, you can set an example by practicing the golden rule in your work and work relationships. Start looking at your coworkers, your bosses, and your company the way

you would like them to look at you. That means understanding that
you are all trying to survive the same "revolution." That means
realizing that there are real people with needs as real as yours behind
that corporate machine. Communication between the real people of
any company is the key to changing a job situation for the better. Once
you begin to understand their needs, it will be easier to make them
understand yours. There are many ways you can facilitate this communication process, and that is what this book is all about.

Remember Kenny at the beginning of this chapter? How long will
Kenny continue to work for a company that seems insensitive to his
family's stability and his health? Other companies may already be
wooing him. Will he simply quit and take another job, depriving his
company of his valuable experience and expertise? Hopefully his
company will be smart enough to realize the cost of losing him if it
doesn't start practicing the golden rule of business.

The statement that best sums up the current job satisfaction crisis
comes from an article in *American Demographics*: "In the 1990s,
understanding workers' diverse wants and needs will be crucial to
turning a profit."[7] In the next chapter, we will analyze these diverse
wants and needs to help you build the best possible relationship with
that lean, mean corporate machine.

The Work Force in Transition: Understanding Diversity

2

According to an article in *American Demographics*, "More than half of the original Fortune 500 companies have gone the way of the dinosaur. Their demise usually followed a natural progression: they did not change, they did not grow, and they finally ceased to exist. . . . Institutions cannot respond to change if they fail to recognize that it is occurring."[1]

In chapter one, we discussed how technology and economics have changed the employers of the work force. And you saw how those changes have made job satisfaction more and more elusive in the nineties. Now let's look at how employees are changing and how employers need to recognize and address those changes if they are to survive the next decade as well. Whether you are an employer or an employee, you need to know how such changes affect your work life in order to survive in today's workplace and be happier and more satisfied in your work.

The Diverse Work Force

The greatest change in the work force today, aside from the technological changes, is in its diversity. What is diversity? Diversity includes many components such as culture, ethnic origin, race, religion, gender, age, personality type, and even physical disabilities. If you went to school during the sixties and seventies, you were probably taught that America is a melting pot. That meant that people of many different cultures, races, and ethnic origins came together and assimilated, or melted, into the American mold. It sounded great in theory, but what our nation began to discover in the eighties and nineties was that people no longer want to be melted into a single mold or ideal. People are beginning to celebrate their differences and treasure the values and experiences that are unique to those differences, whether they be cultural, ethnic, lifestyle, gender, or age.

How does diversity directly affect the work force? These statistics illustrate how the composition of the work force is changing.[2]

- White males represent 45 percent of today's work force; the other 55 percent are women and minorities.
- Between 1990 and 2005, 56 million people will enter the work force; 30 million will retire or stop working.
- About half of the work force entrants will be women and about half will be men, but 57 percent of those leaving will be men whereas only 42 percent will be women. Thus, more women will be in the work force.
- African Americans will be 13 percent of the new entrants; only 10 percent of those leaving. Hispanics will be 16 percent of the new entrants; only 5 percent of those leaving. Asians will be 6 percent of the new entrants; only 2.4 percent of those leaving. Thus, there will be more minorities entering the work force than leaving it.
- Currently, a record high percentage of our population, 59 percent, is in the prime working ages: 25 to 64, whereas the younger work force, ages 16–24, is decreasing. Thus, our labor force is becoming increasingly middle-aged.
- Though human resources practices are still predominantly tailored to workers in the traditional family, in 1991 only 26 percent of our nation's households fit that description. Married couples with no children at home, single-parent families, non-family households, and people living alone have become the larger share of the population.
- Thirteen million non-institutionalized Americans aged 16–64 have a disability that limits the kind or amount of work they can do. Fewer than 5 million are currently employed, but two-thirds of unemployed disabled people want to work, according to a Harris poll.

Those statistics show that the composition of the work force in this country is extremely diverse in terms of culture, ethnic and racial origin, lifestyle, gender, and age. With the acceptance of differences as part of an individual's unique identity, it becomes necessary in the workplace to recognize and meet the needs of diverse people. Systems of recruiting employees, corporate cultures and traditions, education and training opportunities, and even the types of benefits offered must reflect the needs and interests of different people and family groups.

Personality differences is another area that is being recognized by more and more psychological studies. This is a topic that will become the key to understanding many differences encountered in the workplace, and we will discuss it in depth in chapter 4. In this chapter, we will examine how the other elements of diversity affect needs, perceptions, and productivity in the workplace.

Breaking the Corporate Mold

Every organization has a culture within it. This is the set of written and unwritten rules about how to behave on the job, how to treat equals, subordinates, and superiors, and how to advance in the organization. All of these rules serve to fit employees into a specific mold. The cultural mold in your company may go back to a time when white males dominated the corporate structure. Or it may derive from one entrepreneur who single-handedly brought the business into being and expects every employee to have the same excess of enthusiasm, energy, and single-minded dedication to the business he or she has. Understanding this culture, particularly the unwritten rules, can be paramount to your survival in your job. But changing it can be just as critical.

You may believe that overt racial, ethnic, or gender discrimination (including sexual harassment) does not take place in your company. Fortunately, such discrimination is illegal, and most organizations are smart enough to know that. In fact, most companies these days have some kind of Affirmative Action plan and promote Equal Opportunity Employment. But a true sensitivity to managing diversity in the workplace is still somewhat rare. The following are examples of the ways in which misunderstanding of cultural, racial, ethnic, and gender differences can stifle a person's potential:

- A Hispanic manager is told by a superior that he is hot-tempered and prone to violence because of his ethnic background.[3]
- Another Hispanic manager says the Latin culture teaches those in charge to involve others in the decision-making process. Americans tend to think that that is not "taking charge" of a situation.[4]
- An Asian business owner is unable to secure bonding from a state-sponsored minority business program for his computer-consulting firm. The program is biased toward African American construction firms, so Asians tend to be excluded.
- An Asian scientist believes that Asians are stereotyped as technologists, barring them from being considered for other positions and promotions.
- A white female manager believes that women are expected to act like men in order to be effective managers. She believes that women have different approaches to management than men and that those differences should be recognized as having their own advantages.[5]
- A white high school football coach is exasperated by his Native American football team because they don't display enough competitiveness. The Native American boys, raised on a reservation, have been taught by their culture that cooperation is more important than competition.
- An older African American woman, who is the only black person in her office, feels that she is not as good as the other office workers. She was raised in a time and part of the country that taught her that she was inferior to whites. As she continues in her job, however, she realizes she is doing work that is as good as, and even better than those around her.
- A survey in *Working Woman* magazine revealed that women in high-paying upper management and professional positions are more likely to experience sexual harassment than women in lower positions. Sixty percent of those responding said they had personally experienced such harassment.[6]

Such experiences are faced by workers on the job every day. Though they may not appear to be blatant discrimination, they do prevent a worker from doing his or her job effectively and reaching his or her full potential. By the year 2000, when six out of every seven new employees are women or minorities, businesses will not be able to afford to continue such corporate cultures and attitudes.

A Diverse Population Means Diverse Customers

Businesses must also realize that not only are their employees becoming more diverse all the time, but so are their customers. African Americans, Hispanics, and Asians now make up nearly one-quarter of the United States population and command a collective consumer spending power of nearly $500 billion.[7] Women and people over the age of fifty are increasingly predominant in the consumer population, as well as in the decision-making levels of business. Thus, both consumers and business customers are becoming increasingly diverse and present an array of needs and wants for industries to fill. They also bring unique perspectives and values to their buying habits, of which businesses must be aware. It pays to study and research, ask questions, and seek feedback from both employees and customers. Ignoring diversity and changing attitudes toward diversity can only result in the demise of American businesses.

Current household trends indicate that few workers have someone at home to perform traditional consumer activities while they work. That means that more companies must be structured to allow employees to handle personal business on a flexible basis. For example, a divorced mother must be able to accommodate the needs of her children without her work or her children suffering. That may mean flexible scheduling and personal leave time or even the choice to work at home when feasible. Businesses must also offer her flexibility and service to accommodate her needs as a customer. In addition, a record number of workers are having to care for aging parents these days. That often requires as much leeway in the work schedule as parents with children need, in order to keep medical appointments, purchase groceries, and provide other types of aid.

The Top-Down Management Strategy

The hierarchical organization of business is another area that is beginning to change in order to accommodate different lifestyles and perspectives. Since the turn of the century, our mass production manufacturing economy has been organized around the principles taught by theorists such as Frederick Winslow Taylor. Taylorism breaks work down into simple tasks that are repeated over and over, which allows workers with little formal education to follow simple instructions without having to think on their own and to achieve "machine-like efficiency."[8]

Management of this system consists of several levels of bosses who tell each descending level what to do. No one has to think or make decisions above his level of authority. (The term *his* is used here because of the fact that for most of the manufacturing economy, from 1900 to 1960, with only rare exceptions, white males were the bosses, as well as a large part of the workers.) This top-down hierarchy results mostly in "doer" managers who see their workers merely as extensions of themselves, allowing them to "do" more work.[9] In other words, they are the chief doers, setting the example of how the work should be done and giving orders as to who should perform which tasks. The management of people needs or problems is relegated to the human resources department.

Doer managers believe they are responsible for the actual work and its outcome, that employees are their tools for achieving that outcome, and that any failure on the part of workers is a direct reflection of failure on them. Thus, the rigid hierarchy of boss over worker: do what I tell you and don't make me look bad. That reinforces the message to every worker to conform to the company mold and perform only as directed by the boss.

In the rapidly changing technological and service economy, more and more companies are finding that such hierarchy no longer works well. Businesses have become top-heavy with managers whose chief function is to tell the next person down what to do. Manufacturing jobs are being irretrievably lost, but in this era of downsizing, middle managers are also suffering widespread job losses. Along with economic changes, the changes in work force demographics make this hierarchy unsuitable. The concept of fitting into the company's cultural mold is not compatible with a diverse work force who can offer valuable alternative styles, perspectives, and experience to a company's growth and development.

Workers in today's economy must be able to do a lot more thinking on their own than was expected in the past. To be effective and efficient, they must be allowed to utilize all their strengths and talents. For example, look at the white high school football coach who is trying to manage a team of Native American boys. He is employing a top-down strategy by trying to push the boys to respond to a traditional white cultural model of competition. Wouldn't it make better sense to build on their cooperative style and create a strong teamwork model? Instead of trying to instill the goal of crushing the other team, the coach could set a more productive goal for these boys: to rely on each other's strength and support to develop a team capable of performing with precision efficiency. They would be more likely to win that way than by attempting to force "killer instincts" that simply do not exist.

Another example is the female manager whose management style is one of nurturing workers to develop their strongest talents gradually. Her male bosses tell her she is not being tough enough before they've even taken the time to analyze the results of her efforts.

Consider an African American woman writing for a regional news magazine. Her editor believes she is utilizing this woman's talents effectively by assigning her all the stories that pertain to African Americans. Although she may do a good job on those stories, the full extent of her abilities will never be available to the magazine as long as she is limited by her editor's perceptions of her ethnic background.

A Forced Fit Is a Bad Fit

What happens to people who are forced to conform to a mold that does not fit their orientation, whether it be cultural, ethnic, gender, age, or even personality-related? When they cannot "fit in" or perform to the specifications required, they begin to believe they are inferior or worthless. Of course, different individuals react differently, but generally self-esteem plummets, and they actually begin to lose their ability to perform productively. Even when they do manage to fit in by assimilating and covering up their differences, they still suffer from poor self-esteem because they think it necessary to hide their real selves or identities. It is obviously not good business to have employees who suffer from poor self-esteem and are not as productive and creative as they could be. Self-esteem is extremely important to employees' performances and subsequent business success. You will learn exactly how self-esteem affects your job in chapter 3.

The Bottom-Up Management Strategy

How does management structure need to change in order to allow each employee to reach his or her full potential? Many companies are discovering that "empowerment" management is the way to enable diverse employees to achieve their full potential and thus achieve the company's business objectives.[10] Empowerment managers use a bottom-up strategy, primarily focusing on managing people by empowering and enabling them to do their work the best way they can.

Such managers know that facilitating their employees' needs and encouraging them to apply their own skills and experiences to a task, and even to take advantage of new learning opportunities, will result in more satisfied, productive, and profitable employees. There is no rigid hierarchy to keep the manager above the employee; rather, they operate as partners, with the manager saying, "Tell me what you need to do your job well and we'll both look good."

Sensitivity to Diversity Works Both Ways

Being sensitive to diversity runs in two directions. People of different cultures, ethnic or racial origins, genders, ages, personalities, or any other form of diversity should be accepted for their differences. They should not be forced, like the Native American football team or the female manager, to act contrary to what is comfortable and natural to their experiences and perspective. On the other hand, employers must avoid stereotyping on these bases, whether negatively or positively. Managers must manage individuals, not groups. Though they should be open to diversity-related differences, they must also avoid making assumptions about individuals because of a shared characteristic. Only when development of this two-way sensitivity is encouraged and continually developed in an organization through a bottom-up strategy of listening, understanding, and educating can diversity be managed most profitably for both businesses and individuals.

Businesses are also finding that the bottom-up strategy is imperative to surviving in the marketplace of the nineties. They can no longer simply make products and expect people to buy them. They must find out what their diverse customers want and make products to satisfy those wants. Many are discovering that even though there is an excess of workers available right now, they need to develop a bottom-up approach to management if they are going to hire and keep qualified, satisfied, and profitable workers.

A Checklist to Help You Determine Sensitivity to Diversity

Because of legal requirements, blatant discrimination on the basis of race, ethnic origin, religion, gender, age, or disability is not as common as it once was. But even simple misunderstanding and stereotyping can lead to discrimination, which is harmful both to the person who is the victim and the person who discriminates.

The following list of questions is designed to help you gain an awareness of how prevalent discrimination still is in our lives.[11] It is not designed to criticize you or tell who is wrong or right. It is intended simply to heighten your awareness of diversity and the need to be sensitive to it around you. Even one yes answer shows that ethnic diversity is a part of your life and shapes your experience and identity. (Remember that ethnic background does not only mean minorities. It includes any ethnic background such as Irish, German, Italian, Polish, Jewish, and so on.)

1. Have you ever eaten special foods or dishes from your ethnic background or someone else's?
2. Have you ever attended a festival or celebration of a particular ethnic, cultural, or religious group—either yours or someone else's?
3. Do you practice customs or traditions related to your ethnic, cultural, or religious background?
4. Do you ever use words or phrases from an ancestral language, either yours or someone else's (for example, chutzpa or ciao)?
5. Have you ever felt strongly about an issue because of your ethnic or racial background, religion, gender, age, physical condition (such as a disability), or lifestyle (such as marital status)?

6. Have you ever been asked about your ethnic or cultural or religious background or asked someone else about his or hers?

7. Have you ever felt a special sense of relationship to someone or interest in a public figure because that person shared your ethnic, cultural, or religious background, gender, age, physical condition, or lifestyle?

8. Have you ever encountered stereotypes or fixed ideas or made your own assumptions about people based on ethnic or racial background, religion, gender, age, physical condition, or lifestyle?

9. Have you or someone you know ever told a joke related to ethnicity, race, religion, gender, age, physical condition, or lifestyle?

10. Have you ever felt that you or someone else was discriminated against because of ethnic or racial background, religion, gender, age, physical condition, or lifestyle?

Even if you are not an ethnic minority or do not strongly identify with your ethnic background, you probably have had some experience with assumptions made about you based on something other than your individual personality or performance. Whether you are a woman, a single person, a person over age fifty, or even a white male, someone has probably made some kind of assumption about you at one time or another. That assumption may have hurt you, or it may have given you an advantage. Either way, it points out the fact that each of us is different, each of us is a unique blend of many diverse elements, and each of us has a special way of seeing the world and responding to the tasks we perform in it. If that diversity is not acknowledged or encouraged, in order to fit people into the spaces they were made to fill, then we will continue to have a society filled with unhappy, unproductive people.

This chapter should be used as an awareness tool. Make yourself aware of the diversity around you and in yourself. Awareness is the first step to understanding, and understanding is the key to acceptance. In the next chapter we will examine the most important aspect of the business world's diverse human resources—self-esteem.

Self-Esteem: The Basic Requirement for Job Satisfaction

3

If you met yourself in a crowd, what would you see?

One very old book emphasizes the importance of self-evaluation. That book is the Bible and, contrary to what a lot of people think these days, the Bible doesn't teach self-abasement. One of the writers was Paul, who said, "Don't cherish exaggerated ideas of yourself or your importance, but try to have a sane estimate of your capabilities."[1] Other translations say, "Think of yourself with sober judgment,"[2] and, "Be honest in your estimate of yourselves."[3] Paul was talking about the different gifts and responsibilities that God has given each of us. You are encouraged not to have a low estimation of yourself but rather a true one. That means honestly owning both your weaknesses and your strengths.

How do you accurately evaluate yourself, and what standard should you follow? No matter what your personal religious beliefs are, I hope you'll find wisdom in these pages and help for building healthy, balanced, and realistic self-esteem.

Self-image is how you see yourself and how you think others see you, regardless of what you are really like. Self-image can be so powerfully ingrained that it can actually cause people to be physically destructive to themselves. Anorexia nervosa is one good example of that. Victims of this eating disorder believe they are fat, no matter how dangerously underweight they become. It requires psychiatric, as well as physical medical treatment to deal with the dangerously distorted image these people have of themselves.

If you have a recent snapshot of yourself or a mirror nearby, try to take a detached look at yourself and ask the following questions. Write down your answers.

1. If you met this face in a crowd, what would you see?
2. What attitude does this face express? What is this person's attitude toward himself/herself, family, work, home, and world conditions?
3. What is this person thinking? Is he or she thinking happy, expansive thoughts or negative, limiting thoughts?
4. What are this person's work habits? Does this person use his or her time and talents efficiently and profitably or let complacency and disorder rule his or her work life?
5. Is this person uptight or relaxed?
6. Who is this? Describe the person and his or her personality. If this individual could change or modify his or her personality, what would change?
7. What are ten of this person's outstanding abilities, talents, and strengths?
8. What are some of this person's underdeveloped areas?
9. What are three of this individual's personal ambitions? Explain why he or she wants to achieve them.

Now that you have answered these questions, know that your actions, feelings, behaviors, and abilities are consistent with your self-image. The image you hold of yourself determines your success and happiness. Your present self-image is the product of your past experiences, attitudes, and conditioning, including your ethnic, cultural, or religious background, gender identity, age, personality, and physical condition. Your self-image is your mental, emotional, and spiritual picture of yourself. It sets the boundaries of your accomplishments. Nothing can be accomplished that is inconsistent with your self-image.

Your self-image is based on your self-esteem, which is your estimation of your abilities and worth. One dictionary defines self-esteem as "an objective respect for oneself." Another defines self-esteem as "self-respect." If you are going to have a sane or honest estimate, sober judgment, or objective respect for yourself and your capabilities, does that mean you should have an inferiority complex? Webster defines inferiority as "a deep feeling of inadequacy in any given situation usually paralyzing the individual, filling him with self-doubt, and causing him to refrain from activities that would bring about personal growth and fulfillment."

Inferior feelings are not inborn. They are acquired throughout life and they can be overcome, even though the foundations for these attitudes had beginnings that are long past.

Overcoming Inferiority

Whether you know it or not, you project your self-image to other people. Think about your driver's license photo. Do you voluntarily offer to show it to people? You probably feel that it is distorted and doesn't accurately represent what you look like. Are you projecting a distorted self-image to people without even realizing it?

You act according to what you believe about yourself. If you believe that you cannot accomplish a certain goal, chances are you will not achieve it. Is your self-image a sane, sober, honest, objective representation of you and your abilities? Or are you showing people a poor self-image, representing yourself as less capable than you really are?

Where do you get your self-image and self-esteem in the first place? Psychologists explain that your image of yourself is first formed as a reflection of what you saw mirrored in other people's reactions to you. Its primary formation takes place during the first few years of your life and comes predominantly from your parents. Brothers and sisters, other close relatives, and friends also played a significant role. If you were told constantly that you were smart and could achieve anything, you probably grew up believing that you were and could. However, if you often heard, "You're never going to amount to anything," chances are you still hear those words echoing in your mind as an adult, and they will be difficult to overcome.

Are you aware that you play those "tapes" in your head? Do you ever hear a voice in the back of your mind saying "You never do anything right!" or, "You're a failure just like your father!" Maybe it wasn't that bad. Maybe you just picked up subtle messages through comparisons such as "David was always the good student in our family." Once those messages were programmed into your mind, you continued to replay them and react to situations the way you were programmed to react.

The formation of your self-image and self-esteem doesn't rest entirely with other people, however. It also depends on your response to their reactions. Society is full of success stories of people who came from horrible backgrounds. Carol Burnett has had tremendous success, yet she was deserted by her parents at an early age. Oprah Winfrey was raped by a cousin, bounced between arguing parents, and finally left with her grandmother, who often beat her. She has been able to overcome her past and help millions of people in the process. Your personality, environment, culture, and other circumstances of your life will all affect how you respond to the reflection of yourself you see in others. Your self-esteem will also affect your personal and professional success. A positive self-esteem can help you feel effective, productive, capable, and lovable.

Techniques for Building Self-Esteem

Focus on your strengths while you work on strengthening your underdeveloped areas. Learn how to be really good at one thing. Maybe you're a gourmet chef or a whiz with numbers. Becoming skilled in one area will help you build your self-esteem and it will influence other areas of your life as well.

Always remember to be interested in other people. One of the best ways to stop feeling sorry for yourself is to find someone who is worse off than you are and help him or her. More often than not, most people will realize how blessed they are when they help someone who is less fortunate.

To be successful, you need to eliminate old, negative thoughts. Any Olympic winner will tell you that self-talk is important. Remind yourself how capable and worthy you are. You are not an assembly-line creation—you are unique. No one else has your fingerprints, your thoughts, or your way of seeing and doing things.

Don't be afraid to take risks. You wouldn't be where you are now if you hadn't taken some risks and, certainly, you won't be where you want to be tomorrow if you don't take more. Try a new adventure, learn a new skill, or meet a new person. It may change your life.

Fostering positive self-esteem in both children and adults requires the following:

- Acceptance of strengths and weaknesses
- Encouragement
- Praise and taking pride in achievements (even little ones)
- Helping and reaching out to others for assistance and support

- Time to take care of yourself
- Respect for your own uniqueness
- Love for the special person you are becoming

Is Inferiority Always the Reason for Low Self-Esteem?

More often than not, low self-esteem is based on a belief in inadequacy or inferiority. However, many people who are extraordinarily attractive or gifted also have low self-esteem. They see themselves as alienated or cut off from the rest of the world. They may feel as if they inspire only envy and hostility in other people.

How you learn to view yourself depends on your personality, environmental or cultural conditions, genetic makeup and how all those things affect your responses to people and events. Any earlier negative programming can also affect your current feelings about yourself. The computer term "garbage in/garbage out" means that whatever you put in the computer is what you'll get out of it. If a lot of negative programming, or "garbage," has gone into your mind, it will help produce a poor self-image.

That doesn't mean that your parents, or anyone else who didn't adequately meet your needs, are solely to blame for your low self-esteem and any resulting problems. Instead of placing blame, it is more productive to understand the perspective of the other person.

A child doesn't understand or respond to things as an adult would. What may have been logical or unavoidable to an adult may have been devastating to a child's mind. You may have felt rejected, neglected, put down, or unloved when that really wasn't the case. The pressures of a job, family problems, illness, or even ignorance may have prevented your parents or family from responding to your needs. Understand that your parents, teachers, and friends did the best they could, considering their past programming, needs, pressures, and hang-ups. What they didn't give you, they didn't have to give.

Once you recognize your bad programming and where it came from, you can make the choice to change it. Your parents were your most important source of information when you were a small child. You took in everything they told you with equal weight, whether it was good or bad, valid or invalid. But now you can sift through all those comments and reevaluate them for yourself. It may not be easy, but with time and commitment it can be done.

Donald's father was not overly patient with him as a child. He became easily exasperated with Donald if he failed at something. His mother, on the other hand, offered more sympathy and attention when he did fail. Together, his parents reinforced a cycle of failure that convinced Donald early in life that he was incompetent at everything but the most menial tasks. Later in life, his wife's attempts at encouragement were fruitless and even met with stubborn resistance because that pattern was so ingrained in his thinking. It had become his identity, and he actively resented the fact that his wife didn't want to perpetuate it. Donald chose to hold onto his identity as a failure. It was easier and safer than working to rebuild a new identity.

You Can Reprogram Yourself

Whatever your self-image or bad programming, you can choose to change it. It isn't easy, but it is possible. The most adverse conditioning, the worst handicap, and the most crippling self-image can be overcome. I am a living example.

I grew up in a dysfunctional family that provided a lot of bad programming. In spite of it all, however, I maintained a positive outlook. My natural optimism helped me to survive. No matter how bad things seemed, I almost always believed that I would come out on top. But even a positive, outgoing nature can be suffocated by negative input. When an individual is programmed to go against her basic nature by being told, "Don't talk, don't feel, don't trust," she learns to dislike who she is. To make matters worse, my high school counselor reinforced my already shaky opinion of myself. She told my parents that I'd never make it through college.

The reaction to such comments is either to cave in and believe them or to fight. I chose to fight that prediction of failure because that is my temperament. Not everyone has the ability to choose that option, however. You'll learn about the differences in temperament, or personality types, in the next chapter. But I became a high achiever, determined to show those adults that they were wrong. In five years, I had Bachelor's and Master's degrees from Ohio State University, and I even finished my Master's degree with a 4.0 average. But it took me years to realize that I didn't have to perform in order to be accepted. I thought that I was only OK if I was getting straight As, fabulous job offers, and accolades.

Is Your Work Your Source of Identity?

Society reinforces the idea that our work determines our worth. What is the first question usually asked of a man in social conversation? "What do you do for a living?" If he doesn't have the right answer to that question, society wonders what's wrong with him. Women are now experiencing the same problem. A woman who chooses to stay home and care for her children is somehow thought to be inferior to the woman who works outside the home.

During a recent speaking engagement, I was approached by Josh, one of the key people with the company. He told me that in one year he would be retiring and that in his entire life he had never considered who he was outside of his job. He was afraid. He didn't know what he was going to do with his time or his life. Josh is not alone. Millions of men and women define themselves solely by their work. If your work is unfulfilling or boring, your life becomes unfulfilling and boring as well.

A person with a positive self-image realizes that work is an important part of his or her life, but that it isn't everything. It may seem obvious that the better you feel about yourself, the better you will perform, but in fact that isn't obvious to everyone. The key is to cultivate a stable self-image that can handle the bad days without letting self-esteem plummet when failure does occur.

How Your Self-Image Affects Your Job

In 1982, a Gallup poll was taken using a self-esteem scale developed by sociologist Morris Rosenberg. People were asked about their attitudes toward themselves in fifteen hundred personal interviews. At that time, the study determined that about 30 percent of Americans had low self-esteem.

In 1986, the California legislature passed a bill creating the state-funded California Task Force to Promote Self-Esteem and Personal and Social Responsibility. Many other states have followed suit. Why the sudden interest in self-esteem at the state government level?

Officials are realizing the direct correlation between crippling low self-esteem and crime and drug and alcohol addiction.

Rick Gelinas, president of the Florida Task Force on Self-Esteem, said that self-esteem-related problems cause strife in the guise of employee turnover, lateness, and job-related accidents. A more recent poll has indicated that nearly two-thirds of all Americans are suffering from low self-esteem and that that plays a substantial role in economic productivity. The relationship between self-esteem and productivity is of profound importance to business and government.

In 1988, the American Society for Training and Development (ASTD) conducted a study that showed self-esteem as one of the sixteen basic skills needed by employees in the workplace today. The ASTD considers self-esteem a basic skill that is just as important in the workplace as reading, writing, and math.

People with low self-esteem tend to suffer from higher levels of physical and emotional stress, resulting in higher absentee rates on the job. How workers handle stress is a major concern in the workplace today. Stress has become nothing less than a national epidemic.

Marcia Holmes, a fitness and wellness educator who counsels organizations on how to reduce stress in the workplace, believes there is a direct correlation between stress and self-esteem. The higher your stress level, the more out of control you feel, and the more your self-esteem is affected. In turn your productivity is affected.

Symptoms of Low Self-Esteem

People often ask how to recognize or see the beginning signs of an ailing self-esteem. How do you know when your self-esteem is low enough to be a serious problem? One of the most obvious symptoms of low self-esteem is expecting to fail.

Donald, who was mentioned earlier in this chapter, is an example of a person programmed from childhood to fail. Donald always loved history and he knew fascinating things from history that most people don't ever think about. His wife tried to encourage him to go to college and become a history teacher, but Donald was not only sure that he could never get through college, he was also sure that he would never be a good teacher. Instead, he chose to remain in a factory job where he repeated a simple routine over and over. It was a job that never required him to take a risk or learn something new. He held that job for more than forty years and made very good money doing it, but he will tell you to this day that he hated that job. He was safe and financially secure, he was protected from failure—and he was miserable.

Donald is an example of the underachiever who protects himself or herself from failure, but there is another side to this syndrome. The overachiever does everything for the purpose of receiving approval and bolstering a fragile self-esteem. Ruth was driven to achieve straight As in school and perfection in her work because she didn't believe she was acceptable if she achieved anything less. Believing that the more she achieved, the better she would feel about herself, she sacrificed her health and personal life to her workaholic drive. But Ruth discovered that no matter how well she did something, someone else could do it better. Whenever she reached a goal, there was yet another one to reach. And no matter how far up the ladder she climbed, someone else was always closer to the top. Ruth finally realized that she could never be "the best" because there would always be someone better. But she began to see that she could be "her best." She learned to enjoy her achievements instead of worrying that someone else would outdo her.

Low self-esteem tends to project the resulting poor self-image to others. How do other people see Donald? Exactly as he sees himself: a self-perpetuating failure, unable to handle responsibility for his own or his family's life. People saw Ruth as a perfectionist who could never be satisfied.

An obvious symptom of low self-esteem is lack of confidence or assertiveness, but you may not realize that overconfidence and aggressiveness can also be symptoms of low self-esteem. People who are considered braggarts or egotists may be constantly telling everyone how great they are because they really fear they are not. A need to prove superiority, exercise inordinate control over others, or receive credit for even the minutest involvement in projects is often the symptom of a severe inferiority complex.

Adolf Hitler is an example of a man with a crippling self-image. He spent his entire career trying to establish his superiority over others (couched in terms of "the Aryan race"). Tragically, the only way he could prove his and his country's Aryan superiority was to find something that was inferior in comparison. His level of superiority was dependent on someone else's inferiority. This mentality resulted in the near annihilation of the Jewish race and others who were deemed undesirable. When people need to act superior to a person or group because they secretly feel inferior, the result is destructive racial, ethnic, or religious prejudice. Ironically, it is believed that Hitler had some Jewish ancestry himself. Might he have experienced some painful rejection in childhood because of that, causing him to focus his adult anger on Jews?

Maybe that sounds like your boss, who seems to fancy him or herself as a dictator. Try to remember that people who feel the need to be overly aggressive and domineering are most likely suffering from low self-esteem and have chosen the wrong way to compensate for it. On the other hand, the person who never speaks up, never offers an idea, never accepts credit, never protests when people walk all over him or her, has a serious self-esteem problem as well.

A healthy self-image is balanced with a high amount of self-esteem for one's own abilities and worth as a person and enough objectivity to realistically recognize weaknesses and under-developed areas. In other words, you are superior in some things, equal in others, and inferior in others. Compared to every other person in the world, you are "just right." In the chapter on temperaments, you will learn how the various symptoms of low self-esteem relate to the personality type of the individual.

What Is Your Current Self-Esteem Index?

Is there a way to rate your self-esteem? There are a number of psychological tests that will help you analyze your self-esteem and the resulting self-image that you project. Many of them are highly time-consuming and expensive. The following evaluation is fairly quick and simple. It should not be considered a conclusive test or be used for diagnostic purposes, but it can give you an idea of whether your self-esteem tends to be on the high side or the low side. Since no one but you ever needs to see this evaluation, *be honest*, or the test will be of no use to you.

_____ 1. I usually feel inferior to others.
_____ 2. I normally feel warm and happy toward myself.
_____ 3. I often feel inadequate to handle new situations.
_____ 4. I usually feel warm and friendly toward all I contact.

_____ 5. I habitually condemn myself for my mistakes and shortcomings.

_____ 6. I am free of shame, blame, guilt, and remorse.

_____ 7. I have a driving need to prove my worth and excellence.

_____ 8. I have great enjoyment and zest for living.

_____ 9. I am much concerned about what others think and say of me.

_____ 10. I can let others be "wrong" without attempting to correct them.

_____ 11. I have a strong need for recognition and approval.

_____ 12. I am usually free of emotional turmoil, conflict, and frustration.

_____ 13. Losing normally causes me to feel resentful and "less than."

_____ 14. I usually anticipate new endeavors with quiet confidence.

_____ 15. I am prone to condemn others and often wish them punished.

_____ 16. I normally do my own thinking and make my own decisions.

_____ 17. I often defer to others on account of their wealth, or prestige.

_____ 18. I willingly take responsibility for the consequences of my actions.

_____ 19. I am inclined to exaggerate and lie to maintain a self-image.

_____ 20. I am free to give precedence to my own needs and desires.

_____ 21. I tend to belittle my own talents, possessions, and achievements.

_____ 22. I am free to speak up for my own opinions and convictions.

_____ 23. I habitually deny, alibi, justify, or rationalize my mistakes and defeats.

_____ 24. I am usually poised and comfortable among strangers.

_____ 25. I am very often critical and belittling of others.

_____ 26. I am free to express love, anger, hostility, resentment, joy, etc.

_____ 27. I feel very vulnerable to others' opinions, comments, and attitudes.

_____ 28. I rarely experience jealousy, envy, or suspicion.

_____ 29. I am a "professional people pleaser."

_____ 30. I am not prejudiced toward racial, ethnic, or religious groups.

_____ 31. I am fearful of exposing my "real self."

_____ 32. I am normally friendly, considerate, and generous with others.

_____ 33. I often blame others for my handicaps, problems, and mistakes.

_____ 34. I rarely feel uncomfortable, lonely, and isolated when alone.

_____ 35. I am a compulsive "perfectionist."

_____ 36. I accept compliments and gifts without embarrassment or obligation.

_____ 37. I am often compulsive about eating, smoking, talking, or drinking.

_____ 38. I am appreciative of others' achievements and ideas.

_____ 39. I often shun new endeavors because of fear of mistakes or failure.

_____ 40. I make and keep friends without trying.

_____ 41. I am often embarrassed by the actions of my family or friends.

_____ 42. I readily admit my mistakes, shortcomings, and defeats.

_____ 43. I experience a strong need to defend my acts, opinions, and beliefs.

_____ 44. I take disagreement and refusal without feeling "put down" or rejected.

_____ 45. I have an intense need for confirmation and agreement.

_____ 46. I am eagerly open to new ideas and proposals.

_____ 47. I customarily judge my self-worth by comparison with others.

_____ 48. I am free to think any thoughts that come into my mind.

_____ 49. I frequently boast about myself, my possessions, and achievements.

_____ 50. I accept my own authority and do as I, myself, see fit.

_____   SELF-ESTEEM INDEX

To obtain your self-esteem index, add the individual scores of all even numbered statements (i.e., 2, 4, 6, 8). From this total, subtract the sum of the individual scores of all odd numbered statements (i.e., 1, 3, 5, 7). This net score is your current self-esteem index. The possible range of your self-esteem index is from -75 to +75 with -75 being very low and +75 being very high. Yours will fall somewhere in-between. There is no right or wrong score; consider it a beginning reference point to gauge your future progress. Do you need to build up your self-esteem? Does it seem to be fairly balanced? Does it appear to be unrealistically high?

Your self-esteem is not only a product of your heritage, your culture, and your experiences; it is also strongly influenced by your temperament, or personality. The next chapter will show you how to analyze your personality type and how it affects your self-esteem, your feelings about your job, and your job performance.

Self-Esteem: How to Love the Personality You Hate

4

At some time in your life, you have probably asked an age-old question that applies to all kinds of relationships: "Why doesn't that person think like I do?" You may have thought, "That person is just like So-and-so!" or "That person is just like me!" You undoubtedly recognize that there are obvious personality differences among people, but you may never have analyzed their patterns and how those differences affect relationships. As far back as 400 B.C., Hippocrates, considered the father of medicine, analyzed four basic personality types, or temperaments. He based the four types on the predominance of certain bodily fluids: blood, yellow bile, black bile, and phlegm. That is how he named the types: sanguine (blood), choleric (yellow bile), melancholy (black bile), and phlegmatic (phlegm).

Today, we know that personality types are not related to these fluids. But many psychologists do agree that the biochemical structure of the brain is related to the four personality types and combinations of types.

There are numerous tests and systems now being used by psychologists, employers, and sales managers that are based on this four-type model. They use different names for the four types, but they are all based on the same information. For example, Performax Systems International, Inc., analyzes whether a person's behavioral tendency is Influence, Dominance, Compliance, or Steadiness. Those are the equivalent of sanguine, choleric, melancholy, and phlegmatic. The Merrill-Reid Social Styles use the terms Expressive, Driving, Analytical, and Amiable in the same respective order.

Gary Smalley and John Trent use animal equivalents for the four types in their book *The Two Sides of Love*. They are Otter, Lion, Beaver and Golden Retriever. Some systems have even developed rather humorous versions, such as Herbo-Psychiatrists' Pepper, Garlic, Ginger, and Parsley, or Robert Bramson's Exploders, Sherman Tanks, Snipers, and Indecisive Stallers from his book *Coping with Difficult People*. All of these are listed in the same order as the original four.

Because these names and types can be confusing, I have developed a more descriptive set of types for use in my seminars. The following descriptions will give you a brief introduction to each type. I have also included a more detailed test in this chapter, so you can determine your particular type or combination of types. Most people are a combination of two types. Some can even be a combination of three, usually with two of the three being more dominant. You may occasionally see aspects of each type in yourself, but think in terms of what best describes you the majority of the time. If you think all four fit you equally, that may indicate that you feel some confusion about your personality. Perhaps you are not sure who you really are. We'll talk about this later in the chapter.

Are You a People-Person?

The people-person is Hippocrates' sanguine. The original name came from the word *blood*. Hippocrates thought these people had a predominance of blood as they were warm, friendly, outgoing, and generally well-liked. People-persons love people, and others seem to gravitate naturally to them. They are especially known for their talkativeness and love to be entertaining and encourage others to have fun. They are only comfortable in a roomful of total strangers when they can talk to everyone around them, usually asking all sorts of questions and telling their own life story to anyone who will listen. They are particularly good at turning a mundane event into an exciting and colorful story, sometimes stretching the truth to its outermost limits—but all in the name of fun! For that reason they are usually excellent speakers and salespeople.

Because of their openness and warmth, people-persons are sought for help with problems of all kinds. They can find the bright side in almost any situation, and they hate to say no, even if they want to, because they want everyone to like them. Because of that desire to please others, they often find themselves overcommitted.

In terms of work, people-persons find their greatest satisfaction in people-oriented professions such as teaching, counseling, sales, public relations, acting, the ministry, social work, and healthcare. Paperwork and organizational procedures tend to frustrate them as they would rather just deal with people.

To the other personality types, people-persons can appear to be tremendous egotists. In reality, this extroverted, action-oriented temperament, needs to see a response to his or her actions. That means that all of their inner thoughts are almost instantly translated into outward action (especially through the mouth), sometimes resulting in foot-in-mouth syndrome. But people-persons really just need to feel appreciated. A compliment or a pat on the back often means more to them than high pay.

Actress Patty Duke is a people-person. She has led a roller coaster life filled with emotional upheaval, yet she is an accomplished actress, known for her wide range of colorful roles. After being diagnosed as manic-depressive and finally receiving successful treatment, she has been completely open in sharing her personal experiences with others. Her warm, charismatic personality has brought many people to her, seeking help for the same kind of problem. Like most people-persons, helping people gave her great satisfaction.

Are You a Command-Person?

The command-person is Hippocrates' choleric. He thought these people were full of hot, yellow bile because they often seemed to be angry and explosive. Command-persons may seem angry because they are extroverted and action-oriented, like people-persons, but they are usually much more blunt. They are bottom-line, results-oriented people who want to accomplish their goals. Obstacles are seen as challenges to be overcome. Failure is rarely a part of the command-person's vocabulary, but even if it happens, he never quits—he just moves on to the next project.

Command-persons are natural-born leaders—the decision makers, the entrepreneurs, and managers who make things happen. In other words, command-persons like to be in charge. That doesn't always mean they will be the boss, at least in the technical sense. Command-persons can be happy in subordinate positions, as long as they feel in charge of their own projects. They may also feel the need to "give advice" by occasionally telling coworkers how to do their work. If that is overdone too much, however, it can lead coworkers, family, and friends to complain that the command-person is aggressive, domineering, and bossy.

At their best, however, command-persons are great motivators and inspiring leaders. President Kennedy was a command/people-person. During his short term of office, he accomplished a number of goals that had far-reaching effects on our nation and the world, including the space program, the civil rights bill, the Peace Corps, and the prevention of nuclear war. His strong command-person side blended with his accessible and likable people-person side to make him one of the most popular presidents in our history.

Command-persons are happiest when they can fully utilize their abilities to accomplish a goal or complete a project, which they can do best when they are given the authority to direct the project themselves and delegate tasks. Achievement is their greatest satisfaction.

Are You a Detail-Person?

The detail-person, or Hippocrates' melancholy, is the one who wants to analyze and interpret the details. Whereas people-persons and command-persons tend to be bored by details, detail-persons want to know how things come together. Detail-persons are thinkers who like to dig into abstract ideas and theories. They are introverted people who tend to think long and hard about something before giving an answer or opinion. They must be provided with all the facts, figures, and details before making a decision. That may frustrate the people-persons or command-persons who tend to act quickly without putting a lot of thought into their decisions. Neither style is good or bad. Although the people-persons and command-persons may say, "Just do it!" and the detail-persons may say, "I'll have to think about it," each style works well for its personality.

Detail-persons may become engineers, physicists, doctors, college teachers, economists, or computer systems analysts. But they may also choose less technical professions, such as writing or architecture. The key to the detail-person's satisfaction is being able to analyze. He or she needs to create new meanings and methods or improve existing methods and systems.

Detail-persons usually work well with minimal supervision and are frustrated with office politics and poor organization or systems that don't work. They may sometimes be perceived as loners because they are not strong in interactive people skills. That does not mean they don't like people, but they often seem cold and unresponsive because of their introverted nature.

Because detail-persons like to analyze things, they have a tendency to see all the negatives in a situation. That tendency may make the detail-person look like a critic or complainer to the more positive people-persons and command-persons. Each temperament must be seen as adding a piece to the puzzle and creating a whole, balanced picture. Someone has to see the obstacles, and someone has to have the determination to overcome the obstacles. So when the detail-person says, "Here's the problem," the people-person or command-person can say, "You're right. And here's how we can solve it."

Albert Einstein was undoubtedly a detail-person. He was famous for analyzing facts, statistics, and data to discover new theories, including the theory of relativity. But he was certainly not known for his people skills. In fact, he was a very shy man. Like all detail-persons, he was happiest poring over ideas and theories with the freedom and time to analyze and perfect them.

Personality type has nothing to do with intelligence, of course. Einstein happened to be a detail-person with a genius level IQ, but there are genius, average, and below average IQs in all the temperaments. The difference is one of approach, rather than intelligence. Einstein was an analyzer, rather than a decision maker. President Kennedy was decision maker; he let his advisers study the details and summarize them, then he made the decisions. Patty Duke is a communicator. Rather than analyzing her feelings and experiences, she communicates them to people through her acting roles, films, and appearances. Each temperament takes a different approach to life.

Are You a Support-Person?

Hippocrates' fourth type is the phlegmatic, or support-person. This is the person who works quietly in the corner, always seems to have a pleasant response, and never seems to let anything bother him or her. Support-persons are often invisible and taken for granted, but they provide the support structure that keeps an organization going. Support-persons generally prefer to work behind the scenes as they are generally introverted, quiet people. They prefer established procedures and routines. They are usually patient and thorough and often do the jobs that others may find boring. Fields such as bookkeeping and accounting, statistics, engineering and drafting, computers, and skilled mechanical work are often enjoyed by support-persons. Because of their patient, diplomatic nature, they are also good at teaching and counseling.

Support-persons are usually reluctant leaders, but if put into a managerial position, they are good organizers and mediators between people. Support-persons generally dislike conflict; therefore, they are good at keeping things flowing in a harmonious fashion. They like to keep things orderly and predictable. One of their strengths is that they are the steadiest and most reliable of the temperaments.

Though not outgoing, support-persons usually have good people skills. They are rarely the initiator of a relationship or conversation, but once approached, they are usually friendly and particularly empathetic. Support-persons are excellent listeners. They often attract people who either need sympathy or like to talk, because the support-person will rarely be rude or brush someone off. Occasionally, when backed into a corner by a threatening person or situation, a support-person will snap at someone. That is usually a great surprise to the threatener, because it is so rare. One of the support-person's greatest weaknesses is letting others take advantage of him or her.

Support-persons can be incredibly stubborn. They can dig in their heels and refuse to budge, though this tactic is very subtle. Instead of screaming and raging like an angry people-person, barking orders like an angry command-person, or refusing to speak like an angry detail-person, the angry support-person simply won't have your report typed when you want it. Or if the support-person is an accountant, you won't get any of your expense checks until the problem is resolved.

Support-persons are also famous for their delightful, dry sense of humor. Comedian Bob Newhart is a support-person. His early stand-up routines were mainly phone conversations in which he reacted to the supposed person on the other end of the line. His slow-paced, dry reactions were timed so perfectly that one simple word would result in hysteria from the audience. On his television shows, he is always the nice guy whose friends are constantly taking advantage of him. His calm, steady nature and inability to display real anger are often the subject of their jokes.

Support-persons are happiest when the environment is peaceful and without conflict. They gain genuine satisfaction from helping others achieve their goals and receiving the respect and recognition they deserve for their help.

Flexibility and Acceptance Mean Emotional Maturity

The important thing to remember about the four personality types is that there are no strict, inflexible characterizations and that most people are a combination of two types. Even those who are predominantly one type can be flexible and adaptable enough to function in the role of other types when necessary. The ability to be flexible is related to a person's individual emotional maturity and self-esteem. There are times when a command-person can't always be in charge, or when a detail-person has to deal with people, or a people-person has to fill out paperwork, or a support-person has to take over and make a decision. But when self-esteem is weak, it can be a terrifying experience for one personality type to function in the role of another.

Mature, well-adjusted people can accept their own and others' strengths and weaknesses. Though each type has its role to play, some specific traits in each will annoy some of the others. For example, people-persons and detail-persons are opposites who often find it difficult to understand each other. Outgoing, expressive, fun-loving people-persons can irritate introverted, quiet, serious detail-persons. And people-persons may find detail-persons to be picky, critical, and downright boring. Command-persons and support-persons are also opposites. The action-oriented command-person wants to get things done now, but the thorough support-person wants to make sure everything is done by the correct procedure. If each personality does not look at the strengths the others have to offer and the valuable role each plays, they will all have difficulty getting along.

On the job, the effect of personality types can be critical. Many difficult people may actually be in the wrong position for their personality. Is your boss uptight and defensive, stalling constantly on important decisions? Maybe he is a support-person and is uncomfortable with the responsibility. Is one of your coworkers particularly bossy? Maybe he is a command-person who doesn't mean to be bossy but believes telling you what to do is being helpful. The detail-person who appears snooty and antisocial is probably just not good at talking to people.

Approaching detail-persons with friendliness will likely get you friendliness, or at least politeness, in return. It may just take a while to get to know them better. And then there are the people-persons who seem to be in love with the sound of their own voices. They probably aren't as egotistical as they appear. They are just so outgoing and friendly that it's hard for them to turn it off. Remembering those basic personality differences can make an amazing difference in your relationship with your coworkers, especially those who seem to be difficult.

The Romantic Angle

An interesting point about personality types is that, in romance, opposites tend to attract. Though in a work situation, you may work best with those who think like you, you may find that your choice of a mate will be the one who doesn't think like you. Even close friends are often people of opposite temperaments. That seems to happen because you are attracted to something in another person that you perceive is missing in yourself.

Kim, a people-person woman, fell in love with Michael, a detail-person man, because he could explain things in such detail that she understood exactly what he meant. She was fascinated by his careful way of analyzing life as she had never thought of it before. Bill, a command-person man, fell in love with Deirdre, a support-person woman, because she listened intently to all of his ideas about work projects. According to Bill, most other women got bored listening to him. An understanding of personality types also becomes a valuable marriage counseling tool when opposites begin to irritate each other.

Are You Masking Your True Personality?

A serious problem related to self-esteem is the masking of a personality type. Some people learn to put on the outward appearance of a different personality type in order to please a disapproving parent or other significant person. The result is a severely distorted self-image and weakened self-esteem. If someone is telling you, either directly or indirectly, that who you are is not acceptable, you cannot have a good feeling about yourself.

A command-person may be forced to act as a support-person to keep peace in the family. A people-person child may be deemed unstable by a calm, orderly detail-person parent, when actually the child's unbridled sense of fun is simply getting on the parent's nerves. So the child tries to act like a detail-person, stifling his real personality and believing it is unacceptable and unlovable.

Kevin was a bright people-person child who was full of so much energy that his support/detail-person mother just couldn't keep up with him. She finally resorted to keeping him up late at night so he would sleep late in the morning and she would have some peace and quiet. In fact, Kevin's mother was so desperate for quiet that Kevin grew up feeling guilty about his boisterous sense of humor and bubbly laughter. It finally came to a head when a supervisor asked him and another employee to be quiet one day. Kevin exploded and screamed at the supervisor that he was sick of being told to shut up all his life. He wasn't fired for his outburst, but he damaged his relationship with the supervisor beyond repair and eventually had to quit his job. Understanding his relationship with his mother and the reasons for her attempts to stifle his natural exuberance would have helped Kevin to react more calmly to the confrontation with his supervisor.

The same thing can happen when an outgoing parent can't understand why his or her introverted child is so quiet and seemingly antisocial. The child may try to put on a happy face and be the clown, but it seldom works and she becomes miserable trying to be something she isn't. That can also give the child the idea that no matter how she behaves, she is not going to be successful or acceptable.

Leeann was a quiet detail/support-person. As a child she was shy, had few friends, and rarely spoke to adults in the family at all. In contrast, her command/people-person sister was constantly the center of attention. Leeann began to wonder why she couldn't get the same attention. She tried using some of her sister's dramatic techniques but found that adults and other children only laughed and made fun of her. She began to believe something was wrong with her because she couldn't be as charming and outgoing as her sister. A few more instances of being told she was too quiet and too much of a bookworm contributed to severe relational problems for Leeann at school and at work. It took three years of psychotherapy to help her understand her personality and accept the fact that she had as many valuable strengths as anyone else.

The Test You Cannot Fail

Discovering your true dominant personality type and accepting its strengths and weaknesses is key to developing a healthy self-esteem. The following test is designed to help you determine your dominant type or combination of types. There are also numerous other sources from which you can obtain more in-depth information on personality types. A list of sources is included at the back of the book.

One way to tell whether you are masking your personality is to ask two or three other people who are close to you to fill out the test for you. Compare their analyses of your personality with yours. If they are radically different, you may be masking your true personality. You may be telling yourself you are someone else or projecting a false personality to others. Only you can determine which personality is the true one.

Circle all the words in each column that apply to you most often. If you circle a word in one column that also appears in other columns, circle it as many times as it appears. Be spontaneous; try not to think too long about your choices. Then fill in the totals under each column, giving yourself one point for each word circled. Your highest score is your primary personality; your second highest score, or tie score, indicates your secondary or combination personality.

People-Person	Detail-Person	Command-Person	Support-Person
convincing	analytical	adventurous	conforming
cooperative	cautious	ambitious	conscientious
friendly	critical	driving	meticulous
generous	curious	dominant	structured
helpful	independent	energetic	conservative
intuitive	inventive	impulsive	obedient
insightful	intellectual	optimistic	orderly
kind	introverted	demanding	persistent
popular	methodical	self-confident	practical
sociable	precise	sociable	self-controlled
tactful	logical	enterprising	indecisive
understanding	reserved	leader	efficient
open-minded	theoretic	persuasive	patient
service-oriented	experimental	action-oriented	thrifty
imaginative	perfectionistic	frank	humble
impractical	idealistic	practical	modest

colorful	complicated	concrete	stable
expressive	persistent	innovative	down-to-earth
talkative	listener	blunt	empathetic
Total _____	Total _____	Total _____	Total _____

Remember that people should never be judged solely on their personality type. One type is not better than another, and one type is not necessarily better suited to a profession or more valuable to a company than another. Understanding an employee's personality type is no projection of how that employee will perform on the job. Neither is personality an indicator of loyalty, dedication, or moral standards.

If personality tests of any kind are used by employers to screen or eliminate employees rather than to discover the best use of their abilities, they are being used improperly. A personality analysis may be used to support a personal judgment that an employee does not belong in a particular position; that is not its purpose or its best use, however. It is simply a tool to facilitate understanding of how a person approaches situations, problems, and decisions. Use the personality types to help you understand why people do what they do, not to judge them for what they do.

All personality types have strengths and weaknesses. Some people have more of the strengths, and some have more of the weaknesses. Some have different strengths or weaknesses than others with the same personality type. But all pieces fit into the puzzle and complete the big picture. There is a verse in the Bible which illustrates this concept better than any other example:

The fact is there are many parts, but only one body. So that the eye cannot say to the hand, "I don't need you!" nor, again, can the head say to the feet, "I don't need you!" On the contrary, those parts of the body which seem to have less strength are more essential to health; and those parts of the body which seem to us to be less admirable we have to allow the highest honour of function. The parts which do not look beautiful have a deeper beauty in the work they do, while the parts which look beautiful may not be at all essential to life! But God has harmonized the whole body by giving importance of function to the parts which lack apparent importance, that the body should work together as a whole with all the members in sympathetic relationship with one another.[1]

Applying these principles specifically to your job will be discussed in depth in the chapters "How to Love the Coworker You Hate" and "How to Love the Boss You Hate." Now that you've analyzed your personality type, the next chapter will help you learn how to repair a damaged self-esteem, make the most of your particular talents and strengths, and master your weaknesses. You're ready to start "potentializing."

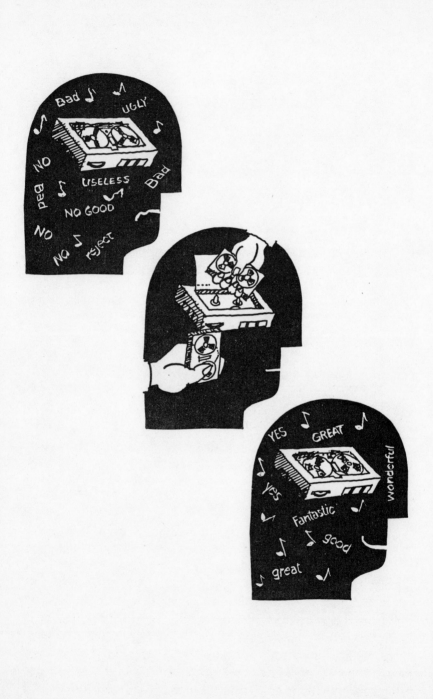

Self-Esteem: How to Repair the Damage and Potentialize

5

How do you begin to feel better about yourself? What does it mean to potentialize? Earlier in the book, you learned the definitions of self-image and self-esteem and you learned how your self-esteem affects job productivity and every other area of your life. There are many different methods for enhancing self-esteem and thus, creating a more realistic self-image. It can be a long, hard process to reprogram yourself, but it can be done.

If you have a serious problem, you should never feel ashamed to seek professional counseling. Most people wouldn't hesitate to consult a professional for a medical problem. Emotional concerns can be just as critical and life-threatening as any disease, so it is just as important to take positive action and seek help.

If you are a parent and you are wondering what you can do to build healthy self-esteem in your children, please remember that you must work on your own self-esteem first. Parents with low self-esteem tend to raise children with low self-esteem, and the cycle often repeats itself from generation to generation.

The American Medical Association published a survey on America's young people titled "How Healthy Are They?" In the past twenty years, suicide tripled among ten- to fourteen-year-olds and doubled among fifteen- to nineteen-year-olds. More than three out of ten adolescents who die are killed in motor vehicle accidents and half of these involve alcohol. Child abuse and child neglect has increased 74 percent in the last ten years. About one in four high school seniors approves of heavy cigarette smoking and one or two drinks a day. One in five approves of trying cocaine. Meanwhile, 80 percent of the parents surveyed think drugs are not a problem with their kids.

That is a sad state of affairs. Why the appalling statistics? Is society in denial? In fact, parents aren't taught how to raise children with high self-esteem. Most adults, many of whom also suffer from low self-esteem, are doing the best they can just to get through the day. In fact, parents will often simply repeat with their children what they heard from their own parents while growing up—playing the same bad programming tapes over and over to their own kids.

In this country, the Society for the Prevention of Cruelty to Animals was founded long before any society for the prevention of cruelty to children. It may seem innocent to assault a child verbally, but that is the beginning of damaging that child's self-esteem and distorting his or her self-image.

Martha had just had her sixty-second birthday. The birthday card from her five children had a cartoon character drawn by each of them. The drawings were impressive. Martha, too, had once been a fine artist, but she hadn't done any drawings in years. Her father had made fun of her artwork when she was a child, and his words had killed her desire to draw. The sting of a parent's words can leave an emotional scar forever. Frequent assaults chip away at a child's self-esteem, ultimately destroying his or her ability to override negative input.

How do you begin to change that repetitive negative pattern? You must change your own behavior. But in order to do that you must change your beliefs about your own self-worth. Unfortunately, many people do not see the need for change until they are forced to by a life crisis.

First Aid for Your Self-Esteem

The following suggestions are by no means the definitive method for boosting your self-esteem, but they are things you can begin to do immediately that will start the process of healing.

Get in Touch with Your Feelings

Remember the old Bob Newhart show where he played a psychologist? He was always telling his patients "Get in touch with your feelings." That used to sound like a meaningless phrase the writers made up to sound psychological. But it is actually a valid need.

A lot of people have learned to wear masks or to create some kind of facade to hide their real personality in order to protect themselves from rejection. The logic is that if someone rejects the mask or facade, at least he or she is not rejecting the real person under the mask. Maybe we think people will like the mask better than our real selves. But the sad reality is that we walk around being rejected most of our lives because other people can't relate to our mask. They sense something phony and defensive and pull away.

Most people who wear a mask aren't conscious of it, though they may know they feel pressured to act contrary to their natural impulses. They may be acting out a personality completely opposite to their own, or they may be clinging to one aspect of their personality that they feel is acceptable and denying other parts of it that aren't.

Introverted personalities are unlikely to express their feelings and emotions, whereas extroverted people simply express whatever they feel at the moment. They tend to speak first and think later. Some people want to analyze or "chew on" their feelings for a while before deciding whether to let them be known or not. Each different tendency has its good as well as bad points.

If a feeling is too painful or too difficult to face, everyone has a way to hide it, either consciously or unconsciously. If you are ever going to begin accepting and appreciating the person you are, however, you have to know your true self. You must learn to recognize reality and take responsibility for it without resorting to denials, defense mechanisms, or other inappropriate coping methods. Inappropriate coping methods include creating a mask or facade, or using drugs, alcohol, or some other substance or obsession for an escape. Any of those things can be used to deny reality in an attempt to try to protect yourself from taking responsibility for who and what you are.

Be Yourself

One of the greatest challenges in life is getting in touch with who you really are. Being who you are may seem very simple, but it offers profound results. And, of course, it isn't always easy! First try taking off the mask with people you are closest to and trust the most. Then try it with others. After all, you are unique. There is no one else in the world exactly like you, so why not be you? That doesn't mean that there aren't some things you might want to change about yourself.

There's nothing wrong with wanting to improve yourself and work on your faults.

Accept Your Limitations

If you are over thirty, your chances of qualifying for the next U.S. Olympic swim team or winning the Heisman trophy are slim. There are some things you can't do, but that doesn't invalidate you as a person. Work on the areas in your life that you want to change, and don't spend needless energy punishing yourself or feeling guilty about your past decisions. When you make mistakes, try to learn from them. Feeling guilty can keep you from taking responsibility for learning from a mistake.

When you do feel guilty, make sure it is valid guilt. In other words, there is a difference between an honest mistake and a deliberate wrong. If you know what is right but you purposely choose to do what's wrong, then guilt is a valid feeling. If that is the case, do what you can to rectify the situation, then stop feeling guilty. Forgive yourself for your behavior and go on. Guilt that continues after you have corrected the wrong is useless and counterproductive. And guilt or regret over an honest mistake is equally pointless.

These initial three first-aid tips are very simple, but they are not easy. They cannot be accomplished overnight. You may need someone to help you begin the process. Look for your sources of emotional support. Where do you give and get listening, love, and appreciation? Who challenges you to be you more fully? Other people can provide much of this support for you as you can for them. If that support seems inadequate, however, never hesitate to consult a professional counselor. The rest of this first-aid list consists of easier, more concrete actions that will help you carry out the first three tips.

Take Care of Yourself

Don't ignore your own needs. Many people confuse self-esteem with selfishness, particularly when it comes to meeting their own needs. Even in religious circles, a myth is circulated that we should not love ourselves. One of the best examples of this is this 5000-year-old commandment from the Old Testament: "Love your neighbor as yourself."[1] It doesn't say, "Love your neighbor instead of yourself."

Author Walter Trobisch calls those words a "command to love yourself" and continues "Self-love is thus the prerequisite and the criteria for our conduct towards our neighbor."[2] Regardless of what your philosophy of life is, you will find that the many books and experts on self-esteem basically agree with this point.

Insecurity and self-hatred will only make you hate everyone else around you. As you are critical of yourself, you will also tend to be critical of others. Adolf Hitler is an example. Being critical of himself, he created the impossible standard of perfection: the Aryan race. No human being, including Hitler himself, ever met the Aryan standard, though Hitler spent his life convincing people that those who did not meet it should be destroyed. That obsession only pointed to his own disappointment with his inability to be the perfect Aryan. He eventually destroyed himself, but the greater tragedy is that he destroyed so many others in the process.

Remember the golden rule of business, stated in the first chapter? This time-honored favorite says to treat others as you would want them to treat you. If you think you don't deserve the best, that you're not worthy of respect or love, are you likely to think anyone else deserves it either? Will you be ruled by cynicism, disillusionment, and resentment? When a person is deeply insecure, he or she may feel jealousy and envy. You may feel so bad about yourself that you can't stand to see someone else get what you secretly think you don't deserve. You measure your worth in comparison to what others have or don't have. If that situation describes you, you're on the wrong track. Remember that you are a human being. Treat yourself like a valid person, according yourself the same dignity, respect, and care that all human beings deserve. That does not mean, however, to put your own needs above everyone else's all the time. That is selfishness. You need to take care of yourself, which means keeping yourself healthy, both physically and mentally.

Today, we hear a lot about co-dependency. To be co-dependent means that you ignore your own needs and put the needs of another person in front of your own. When people are really co-dependent, they can lose their entire sense of self.

You need to remember that your health is your wealth. Without your health, you won't have to worry about all the other areas of your life. You can begin to uplift your self-esteem by eating healthier: cutting down on sugar, salt, and fat. You'll also find that physical exercise will make a difference in how you feel, both physically and mentally. You will find more detailed information and helpful suggestions for these areas in chapters 11 and 12 on physical and mental stress.

Taking care of yourself also includes projecting a healthy self-image to others. It may not seem fair, but people do size you up and judge you by the way you look. Your personal grooming habits definitely project how you feel about yourself. If you look like you don't think you're worth much, with a sloppy, unhealthy appearance, other people may agree with you.

Always remember to take time for yourself. You have needs that are important, and sometimes in order to get those needs met you have to set boundaries around how much you give to others. When you care about people, naturally you will want to meet their needs. You won't mind sacrificing your needs for them because you love them or because their needs are greater. That's loving and unselfish; however, it becomes self-destructive if your entire life is spent catering only to others' demands. When your needs are ignored, it is not only bad for you, but it can breed resentment toward the people you're helping. Ultimately, completely sacrificing your own needs doesn't help anybody. You begin to feel cheated and as though others are taking advantage of you. Learn to say no when necessary.

Get Involved

Get involved with people, with your family, with work, and with others. John Donne said it long ago, "No man is an island." You need people and they need you. Don't hide because you feel you have nothing worth contributing. You especially need to get involved at work today. Think of it this way: if your job pays $25,000 per year, it is equal to half a million dollars paying interest at 5 percent. A $50,000 job is worth $1 million. That's quite an investment! Because of the "lean, mean corporate machine," you're going to have to do more with less. In today's job market, employees must wear a lot of hats and be very participatory.

One of the secrets to success at work is involvement. Start a new project, take a class, learn something new, meet new people, join or start a club or social group, volunteer your time to help someone, or invite some coworkers to your home. You need to invest in your job, just as your employer makes a financial investment in you. You'll find many more ways to invest yourself in your job in chapter 7. Investing yourself in your job and in every other area of your life will pay off with dividends for your self-esteem.

Consciously Visualize a Good Self-Image

Keep pictures in your mind of how you want your life to be. Concentrate on the positive changes you want to make in your life. To change your self-image, you need to change your self-talk and hold in your mind the good qualities that you would like to strengthen. Observe the characteristics of people you admire. You don't want to try to be someone else, but you can learn how to project your best from those you admire. Ask your friends how they have overcome their fears and self-doubts. Then practice the successful methods they have used. The image you put into your mind today will be the image you project tomorrow.

Don't Compare Yourself to Others

Create your own internal standards based on the best that you can be, not the best that others are. Though you may meet someone who looks successful in every way, you would likely find that being in her shoes would involve its own set of problems. No one's life is as perfect as it looks. In fact, she may wish she could trade some of her problems for some of yours.

The key is to accept your differences. It's OK to be a little less experienced, a little less talented, or a little less intelligent than someone else. People are at different stages in their lives, and they all have different purposes. Remember the puzzle. All the pieces are different, but they fit together to form the whole picture. Even the most talented, experienced, intelligent person can learn something from you, because you know things no one else does!

There is a story about a salesman and a janitor at the AlkaSeltzer company. The sales manager was working late one night. He was upset and worried about the direction of the product. Somehow he had to increase sales. The janitor asked the salesman why he was there so late on a Friday night. The salesman explained his dilemma. The janitor asked what the directions on the box said. They were, "Take one tablet, plop, plop, fizz, fizz, and so on." The janitor asked, "Does it hurt to take more than one tablet at a time?" No, it did not. So, the salesman, at the janitor's suggestion, changed the "take one" to "take two" and, of course, doubled the sales. Sometimes people whom we least suspect have the most to offer.

Verbalize Good Self-Esteem

When you talk to yourself about yourself, keep it positive. If you are going through a difficult time, allow yourself a certain amount of time to feel sorry for yourself. After that time is up, don't continue to dwell on it. Begin to reprogram those inner tapes.

Think about when you are the hardest on yourself. When you make a mistake, your programmed reaction is probably something like, "You idiot! You're so stupid! You always mess up." Would you say that to a friend or coworker? Then don't talk to yourself like that. Be as understanding with yourself as you would be with someone else. Say, "That's not like me! I'll get it straightened out. I'll do better next time." In this case, the golden rule is "Treat yourself as you would treat others."

It is also very difficult to project a pleasant attitude to others when you are mentally chewing yourself out. Of course, some people are very good actors. They can fool you into thinking they feel one way when in reality they feel another. In the long run, these people end up with a lot of dishonest relationships and the pressure to keep up a pretense. Your energy is much better spent in projecting a genuinely positive attitude, and that is best accomplished when you feel positive toward yourself and others. Start talking to yourself in positive language, and you'll find that it makes others feel more positive toward you.

Your life will manifest what you believe about yourself. In an old *Star Trek* episode an alien called Gorgan the Friendly Angel kept saying, "As you believe, so shall you do." He used that principle to control the whole ship by threatening people with their deepest fears. Captain Kirk, being a command-person, feared losing command of the ship. All Gorgan had to do was convince Kirk that people were not obeying his orders. He fell apart and ultimately did lose command. But when he realized it was only his belief that he was losing command that was real, he overcame his fear and regained control.

What is a fear or belief? It is not reality; it is only an idea that can have a positive or negative impact on your attitudes and behavior. Gorgan used the crew's fears against them, but when Captain Kirk made them see that Gorgan's power was not real, they no longer believed in him and he no longer had any power.

Your fears and beliefs can have a lot of power over your life. Some of your past programming has had a good influence, but other programming has distorted your self-image. Your task now is to work on reversing the effects of the bad programming. Everything you say to yourself and to others is being recorded in your head, so try to make it as positive and nurturing as you can. Occasionally, constructive criticism is necessary. When it is, remember to criticize the action and not the person.

Accept Whatever Is Valid in Both Criticisms and Compliments

People with low self-esteem have a hard time accepting either compliments or criticism. They take the criticism too much to heart and don't believe the compliments. Look at the criticism you receive; if there is any truth in it, accept what is valid and throw the rest away. When someone gives you a compliment, appreciate it. Compliments are like gifts. If someone gives you a compliment and you reject it, that person is going to think twice before he or she gives you another one. Appraise yourself honestly and accept the valid part of the compliment, but don't let exaggeration or empty flattery distort your reaction.

Make a Think/Thank List.

List all of your blessings, all of the good things that you are thankful for about yourself and your life. Whether you are thanking God or life itself, it helps to realize there are things in your life to appreciate.

Write down your good qualities, accomplishments, and talents. Don't leave anything out. You can add to the list anytime something new comes to your mind. Once you get your list going, use it to help reshape your self-image. Keep all the positive things in your life on this list, including family, friends, work, and home, and keep the list in front of you. Look at it often to remind yourself about all the good things that are in your life. It will help to keep your focus on the positive and away from the negative.

You may also want to write down some of your goals. Most successful people set goals for themselves. Include both personal and professional ambitions. Keeping them in front of you can help you visualize your success. Do you ever wonder where you will be five years from now? You'll be exactly where you are now unless you make a plan for your life. It's like getting into your car with no destination in mind. You'll either get lost or end up someplace you don't want to be, and you'll waste a lot of gas in the process! Use your think/thank list to remind yourself of the goals you have accomplished and the things that are already good in your life. That will help you maintain a positive outlook and make new plans for the future.

What Is Potentializing?

The benefit of repaired and strengthened self-esteem is the ability to potentialize or to achieve your maximum potential for personal and professional success. Many people settle for less than the best life can offer them. They may have a fear of failure, or even of success. They are comfortable with what they have now in terms of a job or relationship, as opposed to delving into the unknown which, they believe, might be worse. Life is a risk and none of us would be where we are now if we hadn't taken some risks. We certainly won't be where we want to be tomorrow if we don't take more risks.

Imagine our nation and American business if people were afraid to take risks and be creative. Potentializing is about an employee who is willing to put in the effort to grow, both personally and professionally. It is a two-way process. When employees work on their self-esteem, talent, and skills, employers must offer support, recognition, and rewards. What do employers receive in return? More loyal, dedicated, and skilled workers, a higher quality product or service, and ultimately, greater profit. Together, as a team, employers and employees can potentialize America into another golden age!

Are You Sure You're In the Right Job?

6

What enables people who love their jobs to potentialize to their fullest? Author Marsha Sinetar explains it this way: "They [are] unwilling to live up to what others in authority [hold] up as standards of excellence. [They] do not pursue a career or do work because of the so-called work ethic or because it is profitable or because their parents or teachers or manager approve, but because it is work that will make them happy and fulfilled."

It would be wonderful if everyone in this day and age could choose his or her jobs according to this ideal. Of course, considering the economy and family pressures such as child care and aging parent care, today's workers can't always expect their jobs to fulfill such an ideal. However, that doesn't mean you have to be stuck in an unfulfilling job all your life. Sometimes you may have to compromise and take a job that is not your first choice but is still on the path to your ideal. And sadly, you may have to give up a job that seems perfect because of economic or other circumstances that are beyond your control.

You can learn, however, to fit all of your job experiences into a kind of puzzle that will ultimately create the big picture that fulfills your ideal. This chapter will give you some ideas on balancing the good and the bad in your job and seeing where it fits into your big picture. You will also learn how to look for definite signs that will tell you it is time to move on to something else.

Take a weekend or a day off, when you don't have a major project occupying your thoughts, to step back from your job and analyze the direction you are taking in your life. You might take a look at your current resume, if you have one, and think about the jobs you have had previously and the job you have now. Have your previous jobs followed a pattern? Have they led down a particular path toward a specific goal? Have you reached that goal? Are you moving away from it? Do you need to set a new goal?

Even if you've been in the same occupation for 20 years, you may decide you want to take a risk and change careers. Or you may decide that staying with what you do best is not only the most practical but the most rewarding. There is no right or wrong choice. It all depends on what is most fulfilling for you and pays the bills.

If you ultimately decide to change careers, there are many good books available on that subject. For now, let's assume that you have chosen not to make a career change. However, you may be seriously wondering if you should make a change. Here's an easy way to help you decide.

How to Analyze Your Current Job

Divide a sheet of paper down the middle. Write your personal strengths on one side and your personal weaknesses on the other. Now divide another sheet of paper down the middle. Write what you like or love doing in your current job on one side and what you don't like or downright hate doing on the other side. They don't have to be in any particular order; just write them down as you think of them. Here is a sample list that was done by one of my seminar participants who was an advertising copywriter.

Personal Strengths	Personal Weaknesses
Good writer	Not a good speaker
Organized	Uncomfortable as a leader
Detail-oriented	Sometimes overly detailed
Precise, accurate	Sometimes overly critical
Can analyze facts, data	Not socially outgoing
Good listener	Don't like pressure
Good observer	Need supportive leadership
Work independently	Sometimes get set in my ways
Enjoy teamwork	Don't like committee work
Enjoy planning	Don't like to "push" people
Enjoy research	Need some structure from management
Enjoy learning new things	Don't handle personal criticism well
Continually study my field	Don't like managing budgets

Job Loves / Likes	Job Hates / Dislikes
Writing ads	Getting quotes on jobs
Writing marketing plans	Having to deal with vendors
Planning strategies	Having to do others' work
Researching clients' business	Dealing with rude or gruff people
Analyzing market data	Not being given enough time
Analyzing clients' needs	Constant pressure to produce
Using research creatively	Having my research misquoted
Freedom to be creative	Presenting to a group
Freedom to work independently	Unrealistic expectations of boss
Working in creative teams	Substituting for receptionist

Now compare those two sets of lists. You'll most likely find that your strengths correspond to what you like to do and your weaknesses correspond to what you don't like to do. It is normal to like what you do well and dislike what you don't do well.

What you like and dislike have a lot to do with your personality type. People-persons love dealing with people and hate doing paperwork. Detail-persons, on the other hand, are not comfortable dealing with people, but will be happier handling details and paperwork. A support-person may be unhappy in a position where he or she must take charge and make quick decisions, but the command-person loves that kind of challenge. The command-person, on the other hand, is bored and frustrated with a position that is structured and predictable.

Analyze your lists carefully. Once you have done this simple exercise, you may realize the reasons for liking or disliking your job. Every job will have some aspects you don't like, but if your lists are out of balance and you are doing a lot of things you don't like to do or are not good at, you may be in the wrong job. If you're doing what you are good at, but you hate a lot of the things you have to do, your job may have changed from what it was when you first started. Perhaps you like what you're doing, but you find problems that frustrate you and keep you from doing your job the way you feel you could.

Once you have studied your lists and determined where your problem areas are, you may want to talk to your boss about how you feel. You may hesitate to do this, fearing that the boss will say, "Find another job!" Some bosses may react that way, but don't let that hold you back from taking the initiative to work out your problems. If you approach your boss with the attitude that you want to do a better job, you should get a favorable response. Most employers appreciate an employee's willingness to make things better on the job and improve his or her performance. Resolving the things that you hate about your job will improve your performance. It is also a lot easier and less expensive for your boss to sit down and talk with you than it is to train a new employee. But someone has to be willing to say, "Can we talk?" and it most likely will have to be you. Even changing jobs doesn't always help, because people who are unwilling to discuss problems are apt to carry the same problems over to a new job situation.

What Are Valid Reasons to Quit a Job?

If your personality and career choice seem compatible but you are still unhappy in your job, are there other valid reasons to look for a new job? In their book, *Before You Say "I Quit"*, Diane Holloway and Nancy Bishop surveyed employers and listed reasons for quitting a previous job that are considered valid and invalid by employers who interview job applicants.[1] Valid or justifiable reasons include:

1. A better opportunity for advancement or a more prestigious company
2. A higher salary (at least 10 percent higher)
3. More job security (fear of mergers, cutbacks, and so on)
4. Starting your own business
5. Moving because your spouse is transferred
6. Seeking additional education (to advance or increase knowledge of your field)

Reasons that cause concern and make employers hesitant about hiring you include:

1. Personality conflicts (seen as an inability to get along with people)
2. Personal problems such as divorce, illness, and so on (seen as an inability to cope with personal issues without allowing work to be affected)
3. Work was too demanding (you may be seen as a chronic complainer)
4. Burnout (seen as an inability to handle job demands)

5. Frequent job-hopping to advance your career (you are seen as valuing your own needs over those of the employer)
6. Protesting company policies (again, you may be viewed as a complainer or troublemaker)

All of the reasons for quitting a job that may be viewed as valid by a prospective employer, except for number 5, are good ones but may not be practical ones during uncertain economic conditions. Unless you are definitely leaving because of number 3 and are sure that you will have more job security in your new job, you may want to think twice before quitting your current job.

On the other hand, all of the reasons that cause concern with prospective employers may be valid for you, even though it would be unwise to quit for any of those reasons right now. That is why this book was written. The subsequent chapters "How to Love the Job You're In," "How to Love the Boss You Hate," and "How to Love the Coworker You Hate" will give you specific tips on how to change and cope with those aspects of your job.

There are, however, some situations that really are valid causes to at least begin looking for another job. (It is never advisable to quit a job until you have another one definitely lined up or have some other adequate means of financial support. It generally takes an average of four to six months to find a new job, but in an uncertain economy it could take even longer.) The following are definite signs that a change of employment is in order:

Your Job Duties Have Changed Radically from When You Were Hired

Perhaps due to reorganization and cutbacks in your company, your position has changed so much that you are no longer doing what you were originally hired to do. Lucinda was a marketing manager in a large regional bank. She handled all the marketing and advertising projects for the city where her branch was located. She loved the creativity and responsibility of the position, and there was no question that she was good at her job. But due to mergers and subsequent downsizing, the regional headquarters in another city began to handle all of these responsibilities. Lucinda was given more and more market research work, which was not as creative and interesting as her previous duties. She began to like her work less and less, since she was not performing the work she really did well. She began to think about exploring other opportunities, but she hesitated because she was receiving excellent pay and benefits and liked her coworkers.

Lucinda realized that pay and benefits are not always the most important part of a job. Her strengths were not being fully utilized and chances were that they would never be again in that setting. The company didn't realize it, but it was not potentializing Lucinda and would eventually lose her. Lucinda was perfectly justified in leaving that job, but she did it the smart way. She began talking to people she knew in other companies and seeking out interviews even if there were no current job openings. That way she was able to discuss possible job changes and test the waters to see what was out there. When a position did become available in one of the companies she had talked with, Lucinda was their top choice.

Your Career Field Has Changed and You Are No Longer Able to Adapt

Due to the technological revolution, many career fields are radically changing. Numerous fields have become almost fully computerized, even the commercial art field. Where graphic designers and illustrators once relied on their drawing and hand skills, they are now required almost universally to do everything on computer. Artists who had been in the business for 20 or 30 years began to lose their jobs to younger workers whose art skills were totally computer-dependent.

Some artists adapted well to the new computer systems, but it was painful for artists such as Ellen and Jack who had worked in an advertising art department for more than 20 years to have young computer artists who couldn't even draw by hand favored over them. Being close to retirement age, Jack chose to take early retirement rather than learn a whole new system at his age. Ellen chose to resign and open her own business selling prints of her paintings by catalog. Both made choices to quit their jobs and pursue other options that made them happier, even though their financial rewards may not have been as great.

If you have been in a career field for many years and find that it is changing more than you feel comfortable adapting to, it may be time to consider other options. Your best bet is to study other related fields and find out how you can adapt your current skills and experience to them.

Your Company or Entire Industry May Be Unstable

Always keep up with the economic and competitive trends in your company and industry, as well as with the technological changes. As discussed in chapter 1, entire industries in manufacturing have been eliminated by economic and technological changes. Read trade and business journals that monitor these trends so you have an idea where your industry is headed. That will allow you time to prepare if things begin to look bleak.

The Political Winds Have Changed and You No Longer Fit In

Sometimes the political atmosphere of a company can change so much with a new owner or new management that you may begin to realize that your work style and philosophy are no longer accepted. You may see tangible evidence of this such as the loss of certain responsibilities or privileges. Or you may notice intangible evidence, such as being passed over for raises and promotions, difficulty getting feedback from superiors, and finding your ideas and projects ignored. If that continues for more than a few weeks and your boss is reluctant to discuss your future with the company, it is usually a sign that there is definite trouble looming. You may have done nothing wrong, but the political winds have obviously shifted against you. It is a good time to start exploring your options.

The Organization's Values Are No Longer Acceptable

Often with a political change, there is also a change in company values. Getting a job done quickly may suddenly take precedence over getting it done right. Procedures may change to the point that they are questionable or even unethical. You might try adapting your values to the new ones, but if they are basically unacceptable to you, you will not be happy doing this. You might also try to effect a change in values or return to previous ones, but don't push so hard that you damage your own image with the company. It's better to explore your options elsewhere.

When you are thinking about quitting, the main thing you need to ask is, "Am I in a no-win situation?" If you've tried going through channels, talking with your boss and being patient, all to no avail, you probably should try to get out before your career, your self-esteem, or your health suffers.

If Quitting Is Your Best Option, Here's How *Not* to Do It

If you do decide to quit a job, here are some don'ts to remember:

Don't Burn Your Bridges

You might feel like telling off a boss who made you miserable or quitting without notice, but that could hurt you down the road. You may need this company or its people someday, not only as references, but also as potentially valuable contacts. Write a letter of resignation, emphasize that your decision is based on personal career needs, and give at least two weeks' notice, offering to complete as much work as possible in that time.

Don't Let Your Work Slump or Broadcast Your Bad Feelings While You're Looking for Another Job

Be discreet about your job search, and continue to produce a high level of quality work. If you don't, you could damage your reference from this company and your image with other companies that contact this one. Doing a poor job and bad-mouthing the company can also get you fired!

Don't Feel Guilty

This is most important. You are only acting in your best self-interest. Your company wouldn't hesitate to act in its own best interest in order to survive. As long as you have given them your best work, you don't owe them anything else, especially if they have not fully potentialized you!

Unless you find yourself in one of the above situations, you have probably made the wise decision to stay in your current job. The next chapter discusses twelve things you can do to help you love the job you are in now.

How to Love the Job You're In

7

When asked the secret of living a long life, George Burns at age ninety-five said, "Fall in love with what you do." He didn't say "Love what you do," or, "Do what you love," but rather, "Fall in love with what you do." That implies an active process. It implies that your relationship with your job is much like a relationship with a person.

How do you fall in love with your job? Let's look at how you fall in love with a person. Granted, there is a sort of mystical quality about the process of falling in love. Most people think it happens by magic. But if you analyze it, you'll find there are some processes that happen when people fall in love.

In the previous chapter, you listed all the things you like and dislike about your job. If you've decided to stay in your present job, your list of likes probably outweighs your list of dislikes, or at least the reasons for staying outweigh the reasons for leaving. Now think about someone whom you love. That person isn't perfect, but you tend to concentrate on the things you love in him or her and minimize the weaknesses. If someone criticizes the person you love, you're likely to come up with all sorts of ways to excuse any failings brought to your attention. In fact, if the criticism is particularly severe, you might even get violent in your defense of the loved one.

When was the last time you defended your job to that extent? Do you still concentrate on the things you like about your job? Or have you slipped into a pity party bemoaning all the things that annoy you about your job? That happens in love too. Some people say familiarity breeds contempt, but familiarity also breeds understanding.

Be honest with yourself. Are you giving too much weight to the things you don't like? Why didn't they bother you when you first started the job? Perhaps it was because you were still caught up in the glow and excitement of the things you *did* like. Now it has become familiar. It's not new anymore. So what do you do? Start concentrating on the good things again. Remind yourself of all the things that you love about your work. Hopefully, the list you made in the last chapter will help you to do just that.

Of course, it's not as easy as making a list. Something has happened to your attitude. Your familiarity has caused you to understand your job differently than when you first began. Now you know about problems and people and boring routines and annoying rules that you didn't know about before. It's similar to being in love and finding that person's hair all over the sink and learning that your love falls asleep after dinner. Now that you understand these things and you have decided that you're still in love anyway, you have to find a way to cope with those annoyances. You have to work on bringing the good things and the excitement back to the forefront.

In order to fall in love with what you do, you have to do something. Most self-help books on the market today will tell you that you have to change your attitude. It is an age-old truth. Even the Biblical proverbs will tell you, "For as he thinks in his heart, so is he."[1] Many job-related books talk about doing this by analyzing your values, setting your priorities, and making your work meaningful in a philosophical way. That's all well and good; however, you need to know what you can do specifically each day to help you fall in love with what you do. Here are twelve specific things that will help you change your attitude and put the spark back into your work life.

1. Do Something Different

You've arrived at work. You probably have an established routine that you follow. Maybe you have devised it yourself, or maybe it was imposed on you. The trick is to vary the routine. Do something different from what you've done before. It may sound deceptively simple, but it can change your whole perspective. It's easy to become bored and apathetic about your workday when you're tied to one routine. It's the same in romance too! "Same-old, same-old" can even get to the most precise and scheduled person.

Try changing things around as much as you can. See if you can come up with a more efficient or more interesting way to schedule your duties. If you have a routine meeting scheduled at the same time every week, change the time or cancel it for a week. Your coworkers or subordinates will probably appreciate a change too.

If your lunch hour or break times are flexible, move them around and go at different times whenever you can. You might find that working while everyone else is at lunch and going to lunch when they get back gives you some quiet time to concentrate.

When you go to lunch, you can use that time to let off steam and refresh yourself for the rest of the day. Make your lunch a "creative" lunch. Leave your workplace. The change in environment will do you good.

Then take a walk or read a book. To get your mind off work and give yourself a cooling down period, read a book that is not work related, such as a novel that allows you to escape the real world for a while. To help regenerate your interest in your work or get a fresh perspective, read a book or trade journal that *is* work related. You may find some new ideas to get you out of the rut in your job.

You may want to visit a museum or art gallery to stimulate your creative thinking. Browsing through a bookstore can also get the creative juices flowing. Listening to music can help you relax. Doing aerobics is good for your mental and physical health. If there is a nice outdoor spot near work, a woods or a park, take your lunch there. Sitting in the fresh air and sunshine, even on a cool day, will have an amazingly refreshing impact on your attitude the rest of the day.

The idea is to do something different, something to break the routine, relieve stress and stimulate your creativity. And don't think that creativity is limited to people who write or draw or make things; it can be applied to any job. Even the most technical-minded computer programmer or precision-oriented accountant can take a creative approach to his or her work. That's what keeps it interesting.

An important thing to realize in your work routine is that not every day will be one of excitement and rewarding fulfillment. Don't view the "off" days as boring. Use them as an opportunity to wind down with routine, "no-brain" activities. Then you can look forward to the days when more exciting things are happening.

For example, Joyce, a market researcher, thoroughly enjoys analyzing research data and turning the results into appropriate strategies to solve her clients' marketing problems. But that is also the most challenging part of her job. It requires her most intense thinking and concentration. Though she loves it, if she had to do that constantly for eight hours every day, she would be mentally exhausted all the time. Therefore, Joyce appreciates the simple tasks of sorting surveys and tabulating data that come first. Likewise, if she had to do these tasks all the time, she would become bored. But the variety lets her wind down between strategy sessions, so she can be fresh for the more exciting part of her job.

One last suggestion: Don't put off doing the things you dislike the most. It's better to put them first on your "to do" list so you can get them out of the way and go on to the things you enjoy. You might even want to come in a little early or stay a little later to get them done and off your mind. If you are a person who likes to put off the less pleasant things, remember that once they're done, they're forgotten. If you do the pleasant things first, the unpleasant ones are in the back of your mind all the time reminding you that they still have to be done.

2. Delegate Something You Don't Like to Do to Someone Who Does

As Garfield the cat says, "Never put off till tomorrow what you can avoid doing altogether." Smart cat! Actually, that can work very well if you find tasks you really hate to do but that one of your coworkers doesn't mind doing. Remember the temperament analyses? Perhaps your people-person coworker wouldn't mind making some phone calls for you, if you, a detail-person, would do some paperwork for her. An exchange of tasks like that can help relieve boredom and stress for both of you, as well as strengthen your working relationship.

You may have an assistant or subordinate who would appreciate the chance to take on a new responsibility. This arrangement kills two birds with one stone because it also helps the person in his or her professional growth. A routine activity that seems an annoyance to you may actually be an enjoyable experience for someone who is interested in learning more about the business and eventually advancing his or her career.

One caution here: Be careful not to dump things on people that could cause resentment and damage your working relationship. Make sure the person is willing to take on the task and that it will benefit him or her to do so.

Once you are relieved of one or two of these things that cause unnecessary stress, you can focus your attention where it does the most good. You can probably even accomplish these minor exchanges of duties without going through the boss, as long as the work gets done and the overall routine is not disrupted. Be sure you take responsibility for the tasks you perform (and the other person for the tasks he performs), no matter who was originally assigned to do it so that the working relationship remains fair and intact.

3. Avoid Getting Drawn into Unconstructive Complaining

There are people in every organization who always have something negative to say, without offering any solutions. You're probably familiar with the type. No matter what happens on the job, even if the situation seems positive to everyone else, these people manage to find something negative to say about it. Even if the boss announces that everyone will get a raise next month, one person will inevitably complain that it should have happened last month!

You should recognize the difference between constructive criticism designed to find a solution to a problem and chronic complaining. Be careful not to label someone a complainer when he is simply an analytical person who can foresee potential difficulties. The detail-person and the support-person both have a tendency to be analytical and cautious. Remember that someone in the organization needs to present that point of view, but, of course, it should not become the dominant theme of every project or suggestion. The person who seems to be unyieldingly negative, without being flexible enough to accept solution or compromise is the one who can be a drain on morale.

The best thing to do with people like that is to avoid getting too involved with them. However, if your boss, an important client, or a coworker is one of the chronic complainers, that's not always possible. In that case, be as cooperative as you can, but mentally separate that person's negative attitude toward you or the job from your attitude. Be sure you see him as the true negative influence, not you or your job. You may even consider that he is probably having as tough a time in his job as you are, or worse.

A kind word and understanding attitude on your part can work wonders for your working relationship and help make your job more pleasant. Saying, "I realize you have a lot to deal with right now, but

I think you're handling it really well," can help diffuse the anger of a person who is ready to launch into a complaint session.

A tactful way to steer clear of listening to gripes about a third party is to say, "I know things have been difficult, but I'll be glad to help you get some of that extra work done." Thus you acknowledge that the complainer is experiencing a problem without taking sides. It never helps to take sides with one person against another when you are not involved in the situation. You probably have to work with both people, so you should stay as neutral as you can. By offering your help with a specific task and not taking the side of either person, you offer a solution that will make the complainer feel better but doesn't add fuel to his or her anger.

Here is a good rule to remember when you receive criticism. There is usually some truth, no matter how small, in any criticism. Look at the criticism as objectively as you can, accept what may be valid, and ignore the rest of it. If you really feel that there is nothing valid in it, bounce it off someone else whose opinion is more objective. If you are a person who has a serious problem accepting criticism, refer to chapter 13.

4. Build Good Working Relationships with Your Coworkers

Nothing can make your work life more unpleasant than difficult coworkers, except, perhaps, a difficult boss. One young woman was ready to quit her job because of problems she perceived with her coworkers.

Lynn thought her workplace was full of cliques. She knew that every time she went on break or to lunch, the others talked about her. She thought they didn't like her because she did her job well, observed proper break periods, came to work on time every day, and so on. But was she actually the topic of department conversation for 52 weeks a year? Had she ever approached her boss and explained her feelings? Had she ever approached any of her coworkers and asked them to go to lunch or to have a private talk to discuss her feelings? No, she simply "knew." She had even tried on a couple of occasions to transfer to other departments within the organization, but because she was doing a good job where she was, her boss was reluctant to see her go.

Lynn finally realized that she had to talk to someone about the situation. It had been causing her undue stress for nearly two years. When she did talk to her boss, it turned out that he was unaware of her feelings but understood and provided some significant feedback. He suggested a number of coworkers whom she could talk to about her feelings. In a few days, it became apparent to Lynn that only a small portion of her complaint was valid. Much of the tension was created by her own tone of voice, body language, and subconscious defensive reactions toward others.

The point of this illustration is that many people imagine they have problems with coworkers. Yet, they have never really taken the time to communicate with people or make an effort to build good relationships. You probably spend more waking time with your coworkers than you do with your families and friends. It is only logical that such important relationships require at least as much effort as you give to your friendships.

Do you have a relationship at work that is particularly difficult? Most likely, it can be repaired. Go to the person and ask him or her sincerely, "What can I do to help us work together more effectively?" Note the emphasis on *I*, not *you* or *we*. Even if the other person is the cause, a non-accusatory effort on your part to change the relationship can soften him and maybe even encourage him to open up and admit his faults too. Nine times out of ten, this approach will work. When it doesn't, don't let that other person's negative attitude affect your own. If you have made the honest effort to work things out and he refuses, it's not your fault. But if a difficult relationship can be improved, you will feel a lot better about going to work every day.

Another way to build good coworker relationships is to initiate some get-togethers, such as going to lunch or going out to unwind together after work. That can be a good way to get to know people better and develop support for each other. You can even share concerns together and look for ways to solve work-related problems. Be careful not to let it turn into a gossip circle or a clique that excludes certain people, however. Slinging mud will only cause you to lose ground.

Starting a support group, an exercise or diet group, or a sports team are all effective ways to build camaraderie and create team spirit. You might point out to management that a basketball hoop, a VCR for the lounge, or a picnic table is an investment in employee satisfaction that certainly costs less than dealing with stress-related illnesses or even replacing people. Those are good ways to include people from other departments as well. Getting to know people you don't normally associate with can help you learn more about the company and make contacts that could be valuable to your career in the future. The more good relationships you build at work, the more pleasant and fulfilling your work life will be.

All of these ideas will be expanded in chapter 9, "How to Love the Coworker You Hate."

5. Build a Good Relationship with Your Boss

More work-related complaints have been directed at bosses than any other object. The nature of the relationship between worker and boss automatically causes friction. After all, it means one person tells another person what to do. That's why bosses need a great deal of skill in handling people, as well as a thorough knowledge of their job. If you have a boss who is deficient in either of those areas, you are going to have problems. As a worker, you also need to understand the pressure and responsibility your boss faces and the stress that causes. Remember, there are two sides to every story.

The key to building a good relationship with your boss is opening the lines of communication and keeping them open. As with your coworkers, you may have to initiate this process. Many people are afraid to approach their boss for fear of losing their job, but your attitude can make it work for both of you. It is better to confront problems in the relationship than to try to avoid them. They will not get better by themselves. Ask your boss for a meeting at his or her convenience. Tell your boss you want to talk about ways to do your job better. Don't set a meeting when you are angry or upset with your boss. Wait until you feel in control of your emotions. Then, offer suggestions and ask for feedback. Don't make demands or place blame.

Your relationship with your boss is such an important part of your work life and job satisfaction that chapter 10, "How to Love the Boss You Hate," will be devoted to that subject.

6. Create Your Own Special Project

This is a great way to feel excited about your job and fall in love all over again. Working on a special project that is all your own can help give you a sense of control and contribution. There are many ways to initiate this. Ask your boss what needs to be done, or enlist his or her support for an idea of your own that can benefit both you and the company. You might propose a new approach to an old problem. You could be aware of a way to save the company money. You deal with things daily that may not be as efficient as they could be, or procedures that are outdated or wasteful. Your boss might not notice these things, but because you work closely with them, you can bring them to his or her attention and make both of you look good.

Be creative and inventive, but above all, be assertive. That doesn't mean aggressive, which is overbearing, pushy, or demanding. Assertiveness means speaking up when you have an idea and following it through with well-thought-out reasoning and support. Once you have made a suggestion, or initiated a project, continue to promote it until you get a definite response.

Kelly had been a top-notch salesperson in a small women's fashion store for five years. The store had an excellent reputation but was starting to lose sales to some of its larger competitors. Kelly suggested to the owner that they do a customer survey. The owner didn't see the need at first, but whenever problems occurred or it was noticed that certain customers weren't coming in anymore, Kelly pointed out how a survey would let them know what was wrong and what they could do differently. The owner finally agreed, and once they got the results of the survey, it was discovered that the store could easily fix its problems. The owner was quite impressed with Kelly's perceptiveness and understanding of customers' needs. A few months later, when sales began picking up, she was promoted to assistant manager.

If you run into resistance and your idea seems to cause more problems than it solves, accept that. Dwelling on the rejection of your idea can damage your performance and your self-esteem. Here is an important suggestion for a special project that is not used or accepted: keep a copy or a written record of the project for yourself. You put a lot of time into it, and you should never consider that wasted. It can become a valuable part of your portfolio or may even become an important contribution to your company or career in the future.

Remember, people will never know the great things you are capable of if you don't tell them. And you will never know how great your ideas are until you try them out.

7. Learn Something New

Human beings have enjoyed learning new things since the beginning of time. The joy of learning and discovery carries a tinge of romantic adventure that will give you a new reason to fall in love with your job. Is there a part of your job that you have always wanted to know more about? Perhaps you need some improvement in a specific area of your work. Why not take a class at a night school or local college? You may even decide to begin work on an advanced degree in your field. You may also enjoy attending professional seminars or becoming involved with a professional organization. There are many good ways to expand your skills and reactivate a stagnant career path.

Perhaps your field has areas of specialization that you would like to explore. College, technical, or vocational school classes can help you do that, or a general career-planning course can help you clarify your career goals. Someone in your own company may be able to advise you on how to pursue a more specialized path or may be willing to teach you some new skills. A good way to ask someone for this kind of help is to offer to help when he or she is overloaded or planning a vacation. If this person feels comfortable with you and believes you have the potential talent, a mentoring relationship may even develop where he or she will guide and sponsor you for this position in the future. All of those things will increase your knowledge of the organization, make you more valuable, and open doors for possible future advancement.

Learning makes you feel like you are accomplishing more, which in turn, makes you feel more successful. You should never stop learning. That is the quickest way to stop growing and begin falling out of love with your job.

8. Get Involved in Community Service Activities through Your Company

There are all kinds of community service organizations and projects that could benefit from the support of your company or a group of people in your company. Why not initiate a project for your company or a group of coworkers? That not only helps you and your fellow coworkers feel good about yourselves and your work; it can also generate excellent publicity for your company.

Here are a few examples:

- Organize a committee to help plan fund-raising events in your company. Use the money collected throughout the year for a needy family during the holidays. There are a number of social service organizations that can match up your company with a family who needs your help.
- Plan a holiday party (it doesn't have to be at Christmas) for people in a nursing home or children in an economically deprived area. Hold the party at your office, or if that isn't practical, hold it at their building, school, or some other public facility.
- You might even want to adopt a particular class at a school. Hold special learning days for them, teaching them about what your company does and how they might plan for a future in your career field. Take them on a special field trip, or out for a picnic on a Saturday.
- It may even be possible to form a cooperative educational effort with other companies. Each company can contribute something to an overall program that enriches the lives of people in less fortunate circumstances. The possibilities are endless.

As an individual, you can volunteer your skills to a nonprofit organization. Are you an accountant? Help them with records and bookkeeping. Are you in advertising or public relations? Offer to create effective fund-raising campaigns. Are you a teacher or a writer? Many underprivileged children and illiterate adults could benefit from your help in learning to read. You can find hundreds of ways to use your job skills creatively to help others and make your work feel truly rewarding.

9. Rewrite Your Job Description

Have you learned everything you can about your job? Do you know how it fits into the big picture or how it functions within your company? If you think you have mastered your job, try to learn about the jobs of people around you. You will find that learning the jobs around you, including the basic entry-level positions, can help you understand your own job much better.

One day when things were slow for Dan, a direct mail copywriter, he was asked to help sort response cards that were returned by recipients of a mailing. Seeing how people filled out the response cards gave Dan invaluable insight into more effective ways to write and design the cards. That, of course, made him a better copywriter.

Rewrite your job description to include what you do best in your job and to include any additional tasks that you can handle in your boss's or coworkers' absence. Include any new ideas, projects, or procedures that you have implemented, plus any new educational advancements you have made. All this should help you see yourself in a new light. You can see how you've progressed since you started the job and how valuable you are to the company.

Perhaps all that you've learned and accomplished throws a new emphasis on certain areas of your job. Once you expand your education and learn new tasks, your current title may no longer be accurate. For example, one position where talents and skills seem to be overlooked the most is that of the secretary. Have you made yourself so valuable that you are now more of an executive assistant?

When it is time for a performance review, or even before that if you feel comfortable doing so, show your new job description to your boss. He or she should see you in a different light as well. It could even get you that title change, raise, or promotion.

10. Create Your Own Personal Mission Statement

You may think you already have an idea of what you want to accomplish in your career and life. But it can be surprisingly helpful and enlightening to write it out. Mapping out a plan that puts all of your life goals into perspective can greatly affect your feelings about your present job. Here are some suggestions on how to write out a personal mission statement.

- Write a brief description of the main theme, goal, or mission in your life's work. Your faith or personal philosophy will have a great deal of influence on this goal. (The statement can be very simple; for example, a nurse might say, "To be especially understanding and comforting to people who are ill and to help their loved ones cope." Even a store clerk or gas station attendant can take satisfaction in his or her work by striving "to be accurate in details and attentive and helpful to customers.")

- How does your job and your company fit into this plan? Does it offer you an opportunity to fulfill your mission? Does it thwart your mission? Or does it give you the chance to overcome some obstacles in your industry and develop strength that will benefit you as well as others?
- Can you do something in this job to help make your company or industry better from within? (A teacher's personal mission might be to give her students a quality education by improving some of the problems in the school system.)
- Where is this job going in terms of your personal goals? Is it a means to another job that will accomplish your mission? Or do you see a chance to reshape things right where you are?

All of these questions can help you determine whether you're on the track to fulfilling your personal goals or whether you need to switch to a different track.

11. Give Yourself Credit for What You Accomplish

Keep a special "me" file in your desk that you can pull out and look at on days when things are going wrong or when you feel unappreciated. The file should contain any awards, certificates, or notes of appreciation from supervisors, clients, or coworkers. Even if someone compliments your work verbally, write yourself a little note about it and tuck it into your file. That is not egotistical. Even if you are the only one to ever see this file, you deserve to be reminded of the good things you do.

Another entry in your "me" file should be an updated resume. Even if you are not looking for another job, keep your resume up-to-date with your current accomplishments and skills. That will help you see how far you've come in your career development. And, of course, it could always come in handy if you do come across an irresistible job opportunity.

Here's something else that can be invaluable in your "me" file. You might call it a "me" resume. It is a list of specific things at which you consider yourself an expert on the job. These are not the kind of things that normally go into a job description, but they become very much a part of the job for you. They are all the little things that count, such as knowing just what to say to a particularly difficult client. Perhaps you have developed a knack for writing up invoices so they get processed twice as fast. You may even be the only person in your department who knows how to change the paper in the fax machine.

However small you may think those things are, they are immensely important to getting the job done. You should gain satisfaction from knowing that they will help the next person do the job and, ultimately, make the company run more smoothly. Give yourself credit. You deserve it.

12. The Myth of Batting 1000: Don't Give Up.

You may try your best to make your job enjoyable, but there will always be things that cause you problems. Not everything you do will work, but does that mean you shouldn't try? Of course not. Did you know that in baseball a batting average of .300, which means 3 hits out of 10 times at bat, is considered great? Babe Ruth's career batting average was .342. That means he had an average of 3.42 hits out of 10 times at bat. Remember that when you are disappointed with your job, with a coworker, a boss, or even yourself. Sometimes, it may seem less painful to say, "If they don't care, why should I?" But in reality, you will feel better if you can say, "At least I care about my job, and I know I'm trying my best." Say that to someone you can talk to and trust. Telling someone else who understands will at least help you feel like your effort was acknowledged. You can also gain satisfaction from encouraging your coworkers who might be suffering through a negative job situation with you.

These twelve suggestions are designed to help you rekindle a feeling of excitement and positive focus about your job. One thing you don't want to do is try to do all of them at once. Set realistic goals for yourself by studying them carefully and deciding which ones you can work on first. Don't overload yourself by taking on extra classes, extra projects, and community service work all at once. It is best to start one project and divide it into manageable stages. Allow yourself to be successful at each stage, and let that encouragement motivate you further.

Falling in love is a continuous process. This chapter provides only a few of the ways you can work at this process to keep yourself continually in love with your job. One of the best descriptions of the process of loving you may ever come across can be found in the Bible. No matter what your personal beliefs, you will find the wisdom in this passage. Think about how these words apply to your job.

> *Love is patient, love is kind. It does not envy, it does not boast, it is not proud. It is not rude, it is not self-seeking, it is not easily angered, it keeps no record of wrongs. Love does not delight in evil but rejoices with the truth. It always protects, always trusts, always hopes, always perseveres. Love never fails.*[2]

George Burns and the Bible can't both be wrong.

How To Love The Boss You Hate

8

Hate—it's a strong word, isn't it? So let's not say you hate your boss. Maybe you wouldn't even say you strongly dislike him or her. Let's just say there's no love lost when it comes to your relationship with your manager; in other words, things could be better. You're not alone in your feelings.

A few years ago, GE did some studies on why their workers were satisfied or dissatisfied with their jobs. They discovered a connection between job satisfaction and worker/boss communication. Five key topics were identified as central to that communication: discussion of work-related problems, informal feedback on performance, informal feedback on salary, career discussions, and performance appraisals.

Ninety percent of the employees who believed the five areas were well covered by their bosses expressed overall job satisfaction. GE's conclusion was that employees who were least satisfied were those who were not well managed. That probably doesn't surprise you, especially if you're working with a boss right now who is less than communicative.

The following quiz is designed to bring your relationship with your boss into focus, particularly in the crucial area of communication.

Circle the appropriate answer to each question, then add up all the circled numbers to come up with the score for your boss.

1. Your boss makes you feel valuable to your organization and to him.
   4—Excellent 3—Good 2—Satisfactory 1—Needs Improvement 0—Unsatisfactory
2. Your boss clearly communicates the performance required for you to be successful at your job.
   4—Excellent 3—Good 2—Satisfactory 1—Needs Improvement 0—Unsatisfactory

3. Your boss clearly communicates what he wants you to do on a
   particular project.
   4—Excellent 3—Good 2—Satisfactory 1—Needs Improvement 0—Unsatisfactory

4. Your boss listens to your ideas and implements them when
   appropriate.
   4—Excellent 3—Good 2—Satisfactory 1—Needs Improvement 0—Unsatisfactory

5. Your boss gives you credit and recognition for your ideas when
   they are implemented and prove successful.
   4—Excellent 3—Good 2—Satisfactory 1—Needs Improvement 0—Unsatisfactory

6. Your boss sets reasonable deadlines.
   4—Excellent 3—Good 2—Satisfactory 1—Needs Improvement 0—Unsatisfactory

7. Your boss makes changes in priorities only when it's necessary.
   4—Excellent 3—Good 2—Satisfactory 1—Needs Improvement 0—Unsatisfactory

8. Your boss makes fair decisions about performance appraisals,
   promotions, salary increases, and bonuses.
   4—Excellent 3—Good 2—Satisfactory 1—Needs Improvement 0—Unsatisfactory

9. Your boss avoids negative confrontations with you.
   4—Excellent 3—Good 2—Satisfactory 1—Needs Improvement 0—Unsatisfactory

10. Your boss considers your viewpoint when making decisions that
    affect you.
    4—Excellent 3—Good 2—Satisfactory 1—Needs Improvement 0—Unsatisfactory

11. Your boss listens to you.
    4—Excellent 3—Good 2—Satisfactory 1—Needs Improvement 0—Unsatisfactory

12. Your boss learns from her own mistakes.
    4—Excellent 3—Good 2—Satisfactory 1—Needs Improvement 0—Unsatisfactory

13. Your boss gives you honest, constructive feedback about your
    work—even when it's not pleasant.
    4—Excellent 3—Good 2—Satisfactory 1—Needs Improvement 0—Unsatisfactory

14. Your boss avoids playing power games when possible.
    4—Excellent 3—Good 2—Satisfactory 1—Needs Improvement 0—Unsatisfactory

15. Your boss does his job in such a way that you can live with his
    flaws.
    4—Excellent 3—Good 2—Satisfactory 1—Needs Improvement 0—Unsatisfactory

Score	Conclusion
60-48	You like working with your boss. You are obviously reading this chapter because it's part of the book—not because you're having difficulties. Count your blessings and use the information in this chapter to improve on a good thing.
47-25	Be of good cheer. By taking an active role, you stand a good chance of creating a more satisfying relationship with your boss. This chapter can help you understand your boss better and seek ways to rectify the existing problems.

24-11   It doesn't hurt to try taking some positive steps, but
               more than likely you will simply need to hang on
               until you can pursue another opportunity. Learning
               about your boss's temperament in this chapter should
               provide you with some coping mechanisms.

10-0   Uh-oh. This could be the main reason why you hate
               your job. Think about leaving your present position
               (if you haven't already), because most likely you're
               in a situation where the best solution may be to move
               on as soon as you reasonably can.

Before you take positive steps toward improving your relationship
with your boss, it is important to understand what a good boss really
is. What, in fact, constitutes good management?

Techniques of Good Management

Here are six points that have been recognized as the essence of good
management. Keep these techniques in mind while you try to develop
a stronger working relationship with your boss.

1. An Effective Boss Builds an Atmosphere of Open Communication

The GE survey mentioned earlier states that open communication
is a major factor in employee satisfaction. You must be able to
approach and talk openly with your boss.

Ask yourself, does your boss have an open-door policy? Is he
accessible, or do you find him reluctant to deal with any problems that
you mention? Is he sending a double message? "My door is always
open, but don't bother me if you don't have to." That is quite common.

An effective manager invites suggestions and even constructive
criticism or correction. Instead of waiting for you to initiate communication, the effective boss may solicit feedback and discuss current
problems and possible solutions. He may have implemented some type
of formal or informal survey process to understand how employees are
doing and feeling about their current jobs.

An exceptional manager cares about the employee and realizes that
employee feedback is critical for the productivity of the organization.
Not every manager is willing to take that time, however. At the very

least, every working person should feel that management is willing to listen. In order to achieve employee satisfaction, goals and expectations must be clarified, and constructive guidance and direction provided when needed.

2. Trust Is Critical to a Good Working Relationship

Is your boss honest and fair? Does he level with you, even when it might reflect negatively on him or the organization? Does he listen to your complaints and respond fairly? Does he follow through on his promises? Has he taken the time to evaluate his own strengths and weaknesses as well as yours?

The best bosses deal with their employees, as they would like to be dealt with. They convey genuine respect by being straightforward in their communications and following through on promises. Your feelings about your work, no matter how insignificant, are important to them. They deal fairly with each employee, not allowing favoritism or personality differences to affect their judgment. When you trust your boss, you are motivated to greater productivity, achievement, and loyalty.

3. A Motivated Environment Must Be Supportive

A boss who says, "We are a team; we work together," creates a sense of security for the employee. Employees are openly appreciated when appropriate and constructively corrected when necessary. They are not abandoned. Problem solving is a mutual effort. A boss will even go to bat for the employee with higher-ups when appropriate. Employees who have that kind of support rarely get into trouble, because they have the direction, information, and tools they need in order to do their job. They also have self-confidence and do a good job, knowing the boss's support is there like a safety net if they make an honest mistake. A supportive boss has compassion and empathy for his employees.

4. A Supportive Boss Has a Genuine Interest in Workers As Individuals

A supportive boss takes the time to get to know each employee's personality, needs, and goals and even to learn something about the employee's personal life.

Such bosses get the optimal performance from each person because they are able to bring out each employee's unique abilities. They recognize that some people need closer supervision than others. They design tasks and working conditions around the individual needs of the employee. Such bosses who are able to make their people feel important and personally significant also generate the most productivity and loyalty.

5. A Good Boss Helps to Potentialize Each Employee within the Organization

A manager should do whatever possible to develop each employee to his or her fullest potential. Goal setting and career planning are integral in this process.

A good boss increases employees' responsibilities and encourages their independence. Creativity is stimulated as opposed to the demand for adherence to rules and prescribed patterns. The boss can take a vacation and not worry about the department coming to a standstill.

The empowered boss knows how much responsibility is appropriate for each employee. She works with her employees and knows their capabilities and limitations without labeling them "incompetent" or "failures."

6. A Good Boss Gives Feedback

Giving and receiving feedback is one of the most important aspects of an employee/boss relationship. Whether it comes from written evaluations, informal or formal discussions, or occasional memos, feedback should be given on a regular basis. How can you know how you're doing unless the boss tells you? A good boss makes sure his people get adequate, timely feedback on what they're doing—right or wrong.

Research shows that positive rewards and appreciation motivate employees and are far more effective than demotivating threats and punishment. That is why bosses who recognize their employees' accomplishments are usually far more effective than those who have a reputation for being tough on their employees. However, when unpleasant feedback must be given, it should focus on the inappropriate behavior, not on the person as an individual. Just because the employee makes a mistake doesn't mean the employee *is* a mistake.

Manage Your Boss for a Change

Many of the major complaints people have about their jobs could be solved at the worker/boss level. A boss who incorporates those six points into her management style can have a positive impact on how an employee feels about his job.

How do you get your boss to incorporate these ideas? By managing your boss. Take an active role in that relationship. Don't wait for your boss to change his response to you—change your response to your boss. Instead of a passive non-response, determine how you will approach your boss based on your understanding of his management style.

You can't control your boss, but you can control your own attitudes, emotions, and work style. Think of yourself as the manager in this case, because you are!

Janet was a bookkeeper in the accounting department of a large company. She was very unhappy with her job and was experiencing stress-related illnesses. The primary source of her unhappiness was her boss, Dave.

Dave was a people-person who would never say no, so he constantly lied about the status of his work. The result was that Janet often got caught in his lies. For more than a year, she tried to hide her negative feelings about her job, assuming that the only thing she could do was wait.

Before she resigned, she blew up and confronted Dave about his lying. In response he almost fired her. She carried her unresolved frustration with her until she moved on to another job.

How do you avoid ticking away like a time bomb in anger and frustration at your boss? It helps if your boss is open to working on the relationship, something Dave wasn't willing to do with Janet. But if your boss seems to be unwilling, remember that your attitude is what's important. A negative, accusatory, or disgruntled attitude will only make things worse. It's also best not to try to approach your boss when you are angry. That only adds to the bad feelings rather than alleviating them.

Instead of smoldering in dissatisfaction, ask your boss when the two of you can talk without interruption. You might say, "I'd like to talk to you about how I can do my job better. I think this could benefit both of us. Do you have some time this week when we could talk? I'd really be interested in your input." That way, it doesn't sound like you want to have a complaint session.

When you go in to talk with your boss, know specifically what you want to talk about. Clarify the issues in your mind first, then write them down. If you need to point out a problem area, especially if it concerns something the boss is or isn't doing, offer a suggestion as to how you could help solve it.

"I know you've been very busy lately and haven't had time to do my performance appraisal. It would really help me do a better job if I could get your input from an evaluation. Maybe I could stay late and take one or two tasks off your hands to free up some time for you."

Remember, too, empathy and understanding is a two-way street. Put yourself in your boss's shoes. Is your boss under a lot of stress? Increasing numbers of managers are suffering from burnout due to the intense pressure they're getting from those above them. Unfortunately, since more and more companies are bottom-line oriented, they don't appreciate the long-term benefits of having caring, people-oriented managers. Your boss may sincerely want to make things better but feels frustrated in his efforts by top management.

Here's where you can manage your boss. Offer support and you will likely get support in return. Believe it or not, he's human too! Ask what you can do to help make his job easier. Be willing to take on some tasks that you may not like; later, you may get a chance to do something you really want to do.

You don't have be a doormat and let him dump all his problems on you. But you can try making an exchange. Maybe his desk is piled high with things he doesn't have time to file. That is just one more stress element that makes him feel that he doesn't have time to devote to helping you. Offer to clear his desk so he will have time to train you in an area you've been wanting to learn.

If you can show your boss that you're willing to give as much effort as possible, you just might earn his respect, even in a difficult relationship. After all, the feedback you give your boss may be just the information he needed to do his job better. Don't be afraid to speak up when your motives are sincerely oriented toward improving your job.

Once the communication ball is rolling, don't let it lose momentum. When you and your boss have set some goals, check regularly to see how things are progressing. You might want to take a few minutes after work once a week to check in. Your boss will know that you meant business and that your efforts were not just a momentary whim.

Here are some other tips to remember when communicating with your boss:

- Develop a specific list of wants that the boss can reasonably implement.
- Turn the tables: give your boss sincere, appropriate appreciation. Make sure it is sincere—people know when it's not real.
- Don't be demanding. If you appear to be unwilling to negotiate about your wants, your appeal will fall on deaf ears.
- Be open and honest. You may walk out of a meeting with your boss without getting all your wants, but you will still have your most valuable asset: your integrity.

On some occasions you may try everything with your boss without getting anywhere. What do you do next? You may want to go to your boss's boss, but be careful about going over the boss's head. It could cause resentment and damage your relationship even further. However, it may be the only way around an immovable object. Don't let yourself be trapped by a boss who is unwilling to give you an honest chance to improve your situation.

Understand Your Boss's Temperament

As you forge a new relationship with your boss, it is important to know his or her personality style or temperament to accelerate the communication process. The following is a brief discussion of the four personalities as they relate to a leadership style.

If your boss is a *command-person,* the best way to communicate with this personality is to be brief, clear, and to the point. Present your ideas as concrete goals, back up your reasoning with facts but not a lot of data, and cite examples of success.

Command-persons are least receptive to anything that appears to be unproductive or a waste of time, including attempts at relationship building that are not related to a specific work objective. They are not interested in small talk. Be as organized and logical as possible in your approach. More than any other temperament, command-persons appreciate loyalty to their policies and to the company.

Jim, a command-person, is the owner of a software company. His bottom-line, results-oriented style of management could be seen as aggressive and insensitive to his employees. But the wise employees have learned to respond appropriately to Jim. For instance, when work on a major project hits an obstacle, Jim's employees know that he sees it as a challenge. Thus, they react by presenting solutions to the problem clearly, briefly, and always with the understanding that failure isn't even in Jim's vocabulary and therefore isn't in theirs. The project will succeed, and Jim (and it follows, his employees) will be happy. This approach applies to working out the obstacles in the employees' relationships with Jim: by mirroring his no-nonsense style, employees see Jim respond in turn with more encouragement and less overly demanding behavior.

If your boss is a *people-person,* be prepared to listen—and listen and listen! People-persons are interested in small talk, especially when they're doing it. Approach this boss in a friendly way, and present your ideas as creatively as possible. Don't deal heavily in facts, figures, or risks. After you've shared your idea, you may find your boss embellishing it with his own. Don't try to cling rigidly to your original idea. Be flexible, and you will be more likely to gain acceptance.

Compliment the people-person on his insight and inventiveness, and you'll find him responsive to your needs. You may also have to drop a few gentle reminders now and then, because when he gets interested in another project, yours may slip his mind. This temperament is the one that will most sincerely want to see you happy, as he loves pleasing people. Sometimes he forgets to follow through, however, because he's off on another idea. Remember not to take that as a personal slight and you should get along famously.

If your boss is a *detail-person,* he is just the opposite of the people-person. This boss expects accuracy, objectivity, and practical guarantees against risk. If you want him to try something new, you'd better provide a detailed analysis of why it should be done and how it will work. The detail-person tends to communicate in a direct, businesslike manner and does not often appreciate a casual attitude or inappropriate humor. He may, in fact, appear curt and cold but is simply more comfortable with facts and figures than polished salesmanship.

The detail boss may not be comfortable in a leadership position. So don't expect acceptance of new ideas quickly or rush decisions. He needs time to analyze things but is very reliable about getting back to you and letting you know how things are progressing. You'll probably find that he actually appreciates communicating with you on a one-to-one basis, once it does not feel threatening. Detail bosses like to take time to get to know you, so your relationship will develop gradually. Just remember to back up your observations with proof.

Leslie is a detail-person designer for an architectural firm. She supervises one employee who, at times, finds Leslie's desire for accuracy irritating and even bordering on compulsive. However, after assessing Leslie's detail-oriented temperament, the employee has been able to develop a satisfying relationship by providing thorough analyses and updates for Leslie on each project they share. The employee also learned that Leslie responds best to direct communication and ongoing, thorough discussion regarding the employee's concerns—especially when the discussion involves practical solutions that are well-thought-out and presented without extreme emotional displays.

If your boss is a *support-person,* he, like the detail-person, may not be comfortable in a leadership position. When trying to initiate communication, be as nonthreatening as possible. Be patient, and take the time to show personal interest and develop the relationship. Don't be abrupt or too businesslike. Support-people are friendly people, but they are not usually outgoing.

It is best to avoid areas of strong disagreement. Support-people do not like conflict. When suggesting new ideas, emphasize your support or the support of other people, he will like supporting other people's ideas. Also, when he has to initiate a change or a project, he needs to know that others will support him. It is easy to get along with a support person when there is no conflict, but he is likely to clam up if you appear disagreeable. He likes to keep things peaceful and harmonious, so he'll usually be supportive and try to help you feel better about your job. Remember that the support person doesn't push, so you may not always get fast action or results.

Most people are a combination of two of these temperaments. Your boss will probably fall into two styles. You can't always identify the secondary temperament, but the primary one should be fairly obvious. The important thing to remember is that, unless your boss is the same temperament as you (which can cause its own problems!), you each have a different way of approaching your job, your relationship, and your life. That does not make either of you inherently right or wrong—just different.

If you are a detail- or support-person, you may be intimidated by a command- or people-person. A command-person may seem rigid, impersonal, and autocratic to a gentle support-person, who only wants to please others and avoid hard decisions. A people-person may seem flashy and impractical to a careful, quiet detail-person who prefers to be factual and precise.

On the other hand, the support-person probably seems wishy-washy and irritatingly slow to the dynamic, hard-driving command-person. And the detail-person can be a dogmatic bore to the enthusiastic, fun-loving people-person.

Think about your reactions. Are you really having problems with your boss? Is he trying to ruin your life, or is he just being the natural-born leader his temperament is designed to be? When you understand your own and your boss's temperaments and how they interact, you're on the road to better communication already.

Each temperament has a function and particular role to play. In managing your boss, remember—if you're a detail- or support-person feeling intimidated by a command-person or people-person boss—he needs you! Who would carry out the commands of the command-person if there were no support-persons? Conversely, who would delegate and discuss projects if there were no command- or people-persons?

Understanding and appreciating differences is vital to managing your boss. You may feel that it is too much responsibility and work to figure out your boss and that your boss should make more of an effort to understand you. In an ideal world, your boss would appreciate your slightest efforts and you would be his number one employee. But in the real world, your goal is to make your relationship with your boss as solid and open as it can be by doing your part.

Now you may be asking, "How can I love the coworker I hate?" How can you learn to appreciate, even like, your coworkers? The next chapter explores relationships among coworkers and how you can turn those relationships, even the difficult ones, into productive and enjoyable teamwork.

How to Love the Coworker You Hate

9

Karen, a junior account executive at a public relations firm, dreads the company's weekly staff meetings. The reason? Rex, one of her coworkers. Rex is also an account executive, but as far as Karen is concerned, that is where any similarities between her and Rex end. She finds Rex obnoxious, opinionated, rude—her list of complaints against him is fairly lengthy. In fact, Karen so strongly dislikes Rex that she avoids contact with him in every way possible, which is why the weekly staff meetings are so uncomfortable. "We are not," she says with a wan smile, "*simpatico*." Despite her ironic tone, there is an edge of despair in her voice—her intense dislike of Rex definitely causes her stress on the job, and she wishes she could do something about it.

In the same PR agency is Chip, a staff pasteup artist, who has his own coworker struggles with Benjamin, a writer. Tight deadlines and high-pressure projects are the norm at the agency, and Chip constantly runs into problems with Benjamin's inability to get the work done on time. Try as he might, Chip cannot get Benjamin to cooperate with him, which in turn hinders Chip's performance. Chip deeply resents Benjamin and is at the point of going to the writer's superior to complain.

Like Karen and Chip, you are contending with a difficult work situation. It is not your boss—you like him or her. It is not your work load—you are handling that well. You are even learning to love whatever other aspects of the job you may hate. But when it comes to that particular person you work with, you may be asking yourself, "Can I ever really love the coworker I hate?" The answer may seem to be a resounding, no.

Yet the answer can be yes, you can love the coworker you hate. But it will probably take some work. Work, because in difficult circumstances, it is never easy to change. Particularly when the person who must decide to change is you.

The work environment can be loosely compared to a family. You are together a substantial part of your waking hours. You depend on one another to meet mutual goals. And you are a group of people with distinct personalities and needs.

As in any family, there are conflicts. But the blood ties and years of togetherness that bond a family together through difficulties probably do not exist in your work situation. So other factors must come into play in order to create a harmonious, productive environment.

With that in mind, let's get more specific to your work environment. Think about your work team now, instead of a family. When you think "team," you picture what *Webster's* calls, "a group of people working together in a coordinated effort."

According to *Boardroom Reports*, "More and more of everyone's work will be teamwork."[1] The future of many of America's companies requires that workers no longer be islands unto themselves but functioning units pulling together for greater productivity and a sweeter bottom line. Even if you are not technically part of a group of people working on a specific project together, you may be looking for the togetherness that comes from sharing a common interest—success on the job. When you make it your goal to work successfully as a team member, you are developing a foundation for success in even the most unstable coworker relationship. It takes time though, as well as your willingness to apply new thinking to the old problem.

Where does that new thinking begin? Here is a list of things you can do to develop a team relationship with the coworker you're struggling to love.

Communicate

This should probably say, communicate, communicate, communicate! That's how important this element is in helping to turn around the negative relationship you have with your coworker. In fact, it is the umbrella for everything that happens as you seek to establish a more positive relationship with your coworker.

What you do and say, and how you look and sound must be consistent and clear. Even if you only talk about work and never get into conversations of a personal nature, you can establish and maintain excellent communication.

For instance, if you have a coworker who seems to constantly misinterpret what you are telling him about what you need, examine your conversation with him. Are you being clear? Are you being direct? Are you listening to his questions, and is he answering yours? Sometimes it is a simple matter of slowing down your way of speaking to present your needs. Do not make your coworker work to understand you; keep your communication simple and to the point. Then his work should improve, which should improve your attitude toward him!

Listen

This is the other side of the communication coin. Let your coworker teach you something about him. Of course, listening involves more than just letting your coworker's comments go in one ear, only to drift out of the other once you leave his presence. Listening means you retain the information, consider it useful and enlightening, and learn about your coworker from what he tells you.

When your coworker sees that you are truly involved in what he is saying, he will respond to you in kind by listening to you. You will discover the give-and-take of true communication, which can only serve to help build a healthy working relationship.

Try a Little Respect

The comedian Rodney Dangerfield is known for his humorous comment "I don't get no respect."TM You may smile at that, but perhaps you should ask yourself, "Would my coworker say he gets no respect from me?" Now, that is not the same as asking, "Does my coworker *deserve* my respect?" Do not place yourself in the dangerous position of judging his worthiness for respect (barring any truly horrendous actions on his part). Simply decide that as a human being, he deserves your respect, which is your consideration and regard for him as a person. That decision can go a long way toward improving your attitude toward your coworker.

Examine Your Own Contribution to Negative Relationships with Coworkers

Examine your own reaction to your coworkers. For example, are you creating conflict that doesn't exist except in your own mind? Are you reacting defensively to a coworker's unthinking comment and letting it fester? The key to making a difference in your relationships with your coworkers is simply to make a move to talk with them and let them explain their position. Again, communicate.

Recognize Your Differences

How do you cope with a difficult coworker? Do you think he is lazy and uncooperative? Does a particular coworker always manage to take credit for your work? Or does he seem to be the boss's pet, always getting the best assignments and privileges, while you languish in a corner with the dullest, most boring work?

Consider this: some of what you perceive about difficult people in your job could be your own inability to recognize that your coworker is simply different from you. Remember the personality types. Though each type plays its own role on a job, some specific traits in each will annoy some of the others.

For instance, people-persons and detail-persons are opposites, and they sometimes find it difficult to understand each other. That is the case with Karen, the PR account executive who has problems with her coworker, Rex. Karen is primarily a detail-person, quietly servicing her clients; she is effective on her job despite a less commanding presence than many others in her position. Rex, on the other hand, is a combination people-person/command-person. His hard-driving, "center of attention" personality seems obnoxious to Karen and, if she were to admit it, a little intimidating. Karen must decide to accept and try to understand Rex's strengths as well as his weaknesses. By focusing on his strengths, she can understand the way he fits into his job and reach a level of comfort in her own.

You should not expect to become the best of friends with a coworker whom you find difficult. Karen and Rex may never go out to lunch as buddies. But if she attempts to understand his personality better, she will be able to learn from him, communicate effectively with him in and outside of staff meetings, and enjoy her job that much more.

As you examine the personality type of your difficult coworker, ask yourself if that person might even be in the wrong position for his or her personality.

Give Up the Need for Control

Whether you're the quiet detail-person or the action-oriented command person, most people who are struggling with a difficult coworker want to do something to "fix" that person—to change him or her into what they think that person should be.

To put it bluntly, forget it! The only person that can change in a coworker crisis is *you*. You cannot expect to control your coworker's behavior without causing further conflict and tension, both for yourself and your coworker.

Chip, the pasteup artist at the PR firm, had to come to that conclusion. He wanted desperately to turn Benjamin the writer into an organized, conscientious person who would help his own job go smoother. But Chip realized that the Pygmalion approach wouldn't work on Benjamin. How can he gain some control over what he felt was an out-of-control situation?

First, he can have a confrontation with Benjamin that is as direct and tactful as possible. Chip has never directly asked Benjamin why he gets behind in his work or told him how his tardiness creates problems for Chip. Instead, Chip has only hinted to Benjamin that there were some problems with deadlines. A more productive approach is to ask questions such as, "How will you catch up?" "What can I do so that there aren't such problems?" Approaching the situation with the team concept in mind—offering a "we" solution to the problem as opposed to a "you" solution—may help Chip resolve the conflict.

Should Benjamin prove to be completely uncooperative, Chip may then chose to seek conflict resolution through mediators, such as their supervisors. Although Chip's initial instinct is to paint Benjamin in the worst possible light, he may find that by leaving the discipline in the hands of Benjamin's superior, he will avoid further tension.

Once you decide to change yourself and let go of your attempts to control your coworker, be casual in your approach to relationship building, as any sudden change in your behavior may breed suspicion.

Your coworkers may begin to wonder, "Now what is she after?" You don't want that to be the response. In an already difficult relationship, the other person may be naturally suspicious of you anyway. Take it slowly and do not make demands. Just let the person know that you really want to work out the relationship to benefit both of you.

Some Other Points to Consider

Praise Has Power

Praising a coworker has the power to change both of you. Unless you are totally unable to find something to congratulate or praise a difficult coworker for, telling her that she is doing a good job can be a true relationship builder. Not only will your coworker respond positively, but you will be reminded about the good things she is capable of, which can create a warming trend in a chilly relationship.

Where's Your Sense of Humor?

Laughter is another power source in boosting a relationship with a difficult coworker. Do you have a shared experience that is funny? Laugh about it together. Do you have a good, clean joke that the other person might enjoy? Open up and tell it. Even when your coworker says something that traditionally annoys you, decide to smile about it and keep on going. (That isn't hypocrisy, by the way; it's self-preservation.)

Empathize

It isn't easy—it even hurts a little sometimes—but try to step into that difficult coworker's shoes. Does he have a boss that irritates him and therefore makes him irritating for you to work with? Is he obviously struggling with personal problems that are affecting his behavior on the job? Empathy can cover a multitude of sins, giving you a deeper awareness of conflicts that could be causing your coworker to be the difficult person he is.

Forgive

As you know by now, one of the main themes in this book refers to the golden rule: Doing unto others as you would have them do unto you. Remembering that concept as you deal with a difficult coworker is vital. When you make a mistake, you want forgiveness. Certainly it takes a great deal of courage and strength to forgive someone if he has damaged you emotionally and professionally, but what a freeing thing it can be to forgive that coworker any wrongs he has done you. Holding a grudge is never productive and only serves to build tension. Forgive and try to let go. You may be pleasantly surprised by the feeling of peace that will most likely follow.

Know When to Cut Your Losses

You hope that you won't have to give up on improving a difficult relationship with a coworker. But sometimes there's just no resolving the conflict. Short of quitting your job, the solutions are somewhat limited. However, you can request a transfer out of the department. You can approach the person's supervisor about the problem and leave it in his or her hands. You can hope that the person will be removed from your immediate vicinity. Or you can simply grin and bear it, keeping in mind that your response can be to respect that person's difference from you, and train yourself in time not to respond at all to his difficult behavior.

On a Positive Note

The Benefits of Becoming a Team

Although it was noted earlier that you will not always, and may not even want to, become friends with the coworker you hate, there is a good chance that you can turn a rocky relationship into a golden one. As you seek to build that team, you can discover some important benefits from your improved relationship.

Support

As author Tim Kimmel eloquently states in his book *Little House on the Freeway*, friends (this applies to coworkers as well) "provide support. They are helping hands and strong arms that help pull us over the rough spots. They are the ones who serve as our search and rescue team when we fall. They join us in celebrating our victories and share tears with us in our sorrow."[2]

Yes, that can happen in your relationship with a coworker. As you both stand on the same side of the same team, you will discover how powerful and effective you can be together, even if you aren't working on the same project *per se.* You will have the added support of a coworker who is open to communication, who is looking out for you as you look out for him. And you can simply breathe easier, knowing the weight of dislike and contention has been removed from the relationship.

Acceptance

Once that bridge of hostility has been crossed, acceptance is on the other side. You accept your coworker; your coworker accepts you. That welcome sense of harmony can profoundly affect your effectiveness on the job.

Openness

Being open means being vulnerable, but it also means you can circumvent hidden agendas, suspicious behavior, and fear of reprisal when you discuss your concerns. When a coworker becomes a team member and a friend, you can expect the nurturing rewards of a good relationship.

Professional Satisfaction

Finally, the decks have been cleared. Now you can get on with the business of doing the best job you can. And if you have been effective in improving your relationship with your coworker, you now have an ally. The work will seem richer and more rewarding when you have resolved the conflict with your coworker in a professional, carefully thought-out manner.

How to Love the Company You Hate

10

Companies, businesses, and organizations come in all sizes and shapes. From massive corporations with international offices to medium-sized companies with a few hundred employees to small business enterprises with less than twenty-five people, the organizational structure, culture, and philosophy is as important to success as the quality of products and services.

Is your company big and tightly organized? Do you have to get permission from your supervisor's supervisor to purchase a few paper clips? Or is your company small and chaotic, with everyone doing his own thing and hoping it all falls into place? Or do you think there is just the right amount of structure, providing adequate supervision and guidance, yet enough freedom to be innovative?

Is the culture of your organization one of strict attention to business, with formal rules and even more formal dress codes? Does it promote some flexibility in how you dress, carry out your duties, and communicate with your supervisors and coworkers? Or is it so lax that it borders on being unprofessional?

What about your company's philosophy? Values? Ethics? Does it put customers first? Does it value and support the employees? Is it concerned about being environmentally responsible? Does it believe in contributing to the needs of the community? Or is it strictly a profit-making venture? Are its ethics questionable in its pursuit of profits?

All of these things must be considered when you are evaluating your feelings about your job. How does your work style fit with your organizational structure? How does your personality fit with the corporate culture? Do the company's ethics reflect your own values or conflict with them? Let's examine each of these aspects of the workplace and look at how they affect your job satisfaction.

Structure: Too Big, Too Small, or Just Right?

Though size was once considered a sign of prosperity and stability for a company, today it is becoming a liability. As discussed in chapter 1, downsizing and lean and mean are the prevalent trends in business now. IBM, Sears, General Motors, Mead Corporation, and many other giants have slashed thousands of jobs in an effort to be more competitive. Layers of middle management have been eliminated to bring decision making closer to the workers.

What does all that mean for big companies? It means the big guys are changing their structure. They are becoming more and more like the medium and small firms that are not top-heavy with bureaucracy. And what does that mean for the workers? It means the people who do the work, who deal with customers day in and day out, will have more involvement in how the company operates and, ultimately, more responsibility for the company's success.

That can have positive results, allowing employees to develop their abilities more fully, stretch their skills, and enjoy the rewards of personal and professional growth. But it can also be scary. If you work for a big company and believe that it is your "security blanket," you may someday find that your blanket has been thrown out. Now is a good time to look at the big picture in your company.

Creating Job Satisfaction in a Large Company

Begin preparing yourself to be more actively involved in the operations and decision making. That kind of thinking could one day save your job if management decides it is cost-efficient to eliminate people who need too much supervision. Here are some suggestions for creating greater job satisfaction in a large- or medium-sized organization.

Always Be Aware of the Big Picture

Exactly how does your position fit into the overall operations of your company?

Know How Necessary Your Job Is to the Big Picture

Does your position involve a level of responsibility that could easily be taken on by some other position? If so, begin to look for ways to increase the value and uniqueness of what you do. The more you learn about your position, your company, and your industry, the more likely you will be considered indispensable.

Learn As Much As You Can About the Positions Around You, Below You, and Above You

If it becomes necessary to downsize and you are proficient in positions in addition to your own, you are the one the company is likely to keep.

Explore Ways to Create a "New" Position for Yourself

Learning new skills, discovering new services, creating new programs or products, or finding new ways to solve old problems that are relevant to your company's business can lead to a whole new set of responsibilities for you. You may reap a new title or even a promotion. Most organizations will be happy to reward innovative thinking in their employees. (The problem of those who are not is discussed in the section on corporate culture.)

Make These Suggestions Part of a Continuous Process

You can never let yourself settle into your security blanket. That doesn't mean you should be constantly fearful for your job, but you will be ensuring a much more secure future in a large organization if you stay flexible and open to new ways to increase your value to the company.

The majority of workers in this country are employed by small businesses, defined as less than 150 employees. Small businesses have their own special structural difficulties. Whereas employees in large organizations usually have some insulation between themselves and the top brass, employees in small companies often have to deal directly with the president or CEO on a daily basis. These entrepreneurial types (almost always a command-person) set the tone for the entire company, dictating how things are to be done and who will take responsibility for them. And, of course, they can circumvent their own systems whenever they wish.

If you work in a small company, you may be frustrated by the seemingly arbitrary control wielded by the top person. Or, the lack of insulating management layers may allow you to work more independently and structure your own position with some freedom. Your perspective will depend upon how organized your company is and how iron-fisted the leader is.

Ted was an account executive in a small public relations firm. The owner was a very outgoing and forceful man who had built his business on his own wits and hard work. He demanded a high level of quality, hard work, and dedication from his people as well. He seemed to prize independent thinking. But Ted found that this man tended to question every decision he made. He was constantly checking up on him to see how he had handled a project. Ted began to think that most of the time his boss did not like the way Ted handled his project.

After receiving much verbal criticism and revision of his work, Ted finally quit making decisions and taking responsibility for his projects. He waited for his boss's input and then let his support people carry out the details. The boss's behavior sabotaged Ted's ability to work independently, in effect handcuffing his employee.

Creating Job Satisfaction in a Small Company

The following suggestions will help you develop greater job satisfaction within the structure of a small company.

Understand the Nature of Entrepreneurs

As the above example shows, it can be difficult to work with entrepreneurs who run small businesses. If you must deal with this type of personality on a daily basis, refer to the chapter on "How to Love the Boss You Hate." It helps to remember that most entrepreneurs are some combination of command-person and people-person when dealing with them (especially if you are a different personality type).

Always Do Your Job the Way You Feel Is Best

Even though the entrepreneur may decide to change a project once you've done it, you should always do it the best way you know how from the beginning. If you try to second-guess someone else in order to do a job the way you think that person would do it, you will likely end up with a result that neither of you finds satisfactory. You will do the best job when you approach it from your strengths and skills, not someone else's. Even if it is changed, you know that you have done your best work. And if the altered version fails, whether or not she admits it, at least the boss will know that your original recommendation may have been better.

Learn to Be Flexible and Adaptable to Almost Any Circumstance

In smaller businesses, things often change quickly. Because there is not a lot of bureaucracy, it is often easy for a small business to react quickly to a sudden market opportunity. That means a lot of work may be last-minute, without adequate time to prepare or go through the proper organizational channels. If you are one of the more outgoing personalities, command-persons and people-persons, you may not mind that. It may seem like an exciting challenge. But for detail-persons and support-persons, the more organized and thorough personalities, it can be exasperating. For the sake of your sanity and your stress level, you must learn to be flexible.

Organizational systems also tend to change frequently and are ignored or circumvented. Because there are less layers to go through, it is easier for projects to go from A to Z without going through established channels. If you are uncomfortable in that kind of structural atmosphere, you may want to consider finding a job in a larger organization. Otherwise, adaptability is your only hope of coping.

Communicate Directly and Openly with Your Boss and Coworkers

In small companies, gossip and rumors circulate quickly and tend to reach the very people they are meant to avoid. It is always best to discuss problems directly with the people concerned. If they hear it through the grapevine, a tense situation will only get worse. Remember to approach a discussion of a concern with a positive attitude, such as, "Because that job was not put through the normal channels, I was unable to get the information I needed to complete it on time. Is there a way we can prevent that from happening when a job has to be done quickly?" The key is to discuss the solution to the problem, not the behavior of an individual. Assigning blame only puts people on the defensive and does not solve the problem. Even if others in the organization put the emphasis on blaming, you can help steer away from it by continuing to focus on the potential solutions.

Look for Ways to Enhance the Value of Your Position

In the looser structure of small companies, there is often a great deal of flexibility in job descriptions. Take every opportunity to learn more about your job and your field. Look for ways to expand your responsibilities. Look for ways you can improve the systems and quality of the company's output. You may even create a new position for yourself. You will achieve greater satisfaction on the job when you allow yourself to stretch and grow. Your entrepreneurial boss will also look favorably on your creativity and drive (as long as you don't take too much of the spotlight away from him or her) because it enhances your value to the company.

Culture: Too Political, Too Conservative, or Comfortable?

You might say the culture of an organization is its personality, or emotional atmosphere. This personality is determined by the relationships in the company—who talks to whom, who listens to whom, and who makes the ultimate decisions. As Alan M. Webber, writing in the *Harvard Business Review* said, "For an accurate picture of how work really gets done in any company, don't look at the organization chart. Map the company's conversation flows."[1]

The larger and more bureaucratic an organization is, usually the more formal and structured its culture is. Though there are certainly exceptions, these are the companies where employees wear business suits and address their bosses as "Mr." or "Ms." People tend to follow the structural systems more closely and stick to the organizational hierarchy in communication. Of course, in every corporate culture there is an unwritten hierarchy and code of behavior known as office politics. Once you have been with an organization for a while, you learn who has the real power, who is the dead weight, and who must be acknowledged from a political standpoint.

Priscilla worked in a multimillion dollar corporation that produced computer software. She was in charge of new product development and was responsible for evaluating or originating new ideas for marketable software products. Though Priscilla was technically in charge of this function, she had been with the company long enough to realize that getting her recommendations to the production stage required the acceptance of a marketing executive who did not share her understanding of the products.

At first, Priscilla was highly frustrated by this fact, feeling that the man was simply exercising some political clout that he had with top management. She even believed that the situation was caused by a sexual bias on the part of top management. That made her particularly angry, considering she was far better qualified to judge new products than the marketing executive.

But Priscilla had to make a choice. Should she protest the situation, threatening to charge sexual discrimination? In fact, her position was superior to the marketing executive's, in terms of organizational hierarchy, so she knew she would have a tough time proving discrimination. Her subordination to the marketing exec was really political, or unofficial, so she decided that building a good relationship with him would be a better way to handle the problem.

It turned out that Priscilla's strategy was a good one. By asking for this man's input before even presenting recommendations to top management, she was able to gain his acceptance on any project she put forth. That also helped her gain approval from the ultimate decision makers more quickly. Apparently the man was a longtime employee who wanted to be recognized as having some authority. Priscilla's acknowledgment of that unofficial authority, which helped move her projects through, was "politically" a smart move for her. In a year the man retired, giving Priscilla free reign and allowing her to fit into the corporate culture in the eyes of top management.

In smaller businesses, the culture is usually shaped by the personality of the company's key leader. At one direct mail company, the president dressed daily in blue jeans and a sweatshirt. He ran the company as if it were a family, with everyone being free to be comfortable in his or her own work style. When clients were to visit, a memo was passed around the day before, and everyone dressed up for the impending visit. At another small marketing firm, the president was insistent that everyone dress professionally. Employees were even sent to seminars to learn how to present a professional image.

The politics in small companies can be just as complicated as in large corporations, perhaps even more so. Structural systems are usually not as strictly adhered to in smaller organizations, so it is easier for idiosyncracies to develop. Although relationships are important in big companies, they are critical in small ones, as you do not have the insulating layers of management to protect you. You may find yourself duking it out directly with the CEO if you do not follow the unofficial politics of getting things accepted.

Coping with the Company's Culture

Following is a list of helpful suggestions for analyzing and coping with the culture of your organization. Most of them are applicable to any size company.

Adapt Your Personality to That of Your Company

Unless the culture in your company is truly intolerable, you will do best to adapt yourself to it and play by the unwritten rules. I am not talking about ethical issues here; those will be discussed in the next section. In this case, we are talking about traditions, pecking orders, seats of power, and how that power is motivated to take action.

As Robert M. Hochheiser advises in his book *If You Want Guarantees, Buy a Toaster,* "Observe your bosses . . . figure out their likes and dislikes, and . . . give them what *they* want without sacrificing what *you* want."[2] That could mean something as simple as dressing the way the company prescribes, or it could mean learning, as Priscilla did, to involve the right people in getting your work accepted.

Be Willing to Make Some Compromises to Accomplish Your Own Goals

You may have to be willing to accept a compromise in order to get some of your goals accomplished. If you are trying to institute a program and you are experiencing resistance from certain factions in the company, you may have to work out a compromise with them. Find out what you can do for them that may facilitate their cooperation with you. Perhaps your program would eliminate something for which they are responsible. Or they may fear other changes that would affect them if your program were adopted. As long as you are flexible enough to understand other perspectives, you can generally work out a compromise that is satisfactory for everyone.

Be Aware of Destructive Cultural Patterns in Your Organization

Some organizational cultures harbor traditions that are based on destructive ideas. For example, the glass ceiling often experienced by women and minorities is an unwritten rule that says some people don't belong in the upper ranks of management. If you are encountering cultural patterns like that, you should first try to discuss them with a trusted colleague. Get an objective point of view on the problem; for example, do others think it is an accurate appraisal of the situation? Once you feel sure about that, it should be brought to the attention of the human resources people. If your company is unwilling to resolve or acknowledge the problem, you may want to consider leaving or even pursue outside legal counsel.

Another type of destructive cultural pattern is the "addictive" organization. Anne Wilson Schaef and Diane Fassel wrote a book entitled *The Addictive Organization* based on the dynamics of addictive behavior. According to Schaef and Fassel, many organizations function in the same pattern as alcoholics and their codependents. Defining an addiction as "any substance or process that has taken over our lives and over which we are powerless,"[3] the authors discuss organizational addiction in different forms.

Often a key person is the addict. (Remember, addiction doesn't have to be a substance; it can also be a process, such as workaholism.) People who grew up in addictive families may replay their codependent behavior in the workplace. Some people may even become addicted to the organization itself.

Dave is the owner of a small financial planning company. Dave is the key person who functions as an addict, with his company as codependents. He is a self-taught financial planner who has built up a successful business in a relatively few years. He is a dynamic people-person/command-person with enough drive and ambition to make up for his lack of experience. His enthusiasm for the investment world has been enough to convince some impressive clients to do business with him.

Dave has also managed to hire excellent employees who have a great deal of experience in financial planning. However, Dave's company experiences an incredible turnover rate: in a company of 10 current employees, 11 people have left or been fired in the last four years! Turnover involved everyone from the receptionist to the senior vice president. What is the problem in Dave's company?

Dave functions like an addict, though his addiction may be hard to pinpoint. It could be a need for success and attention, a need for constant excitement (or chaos, as his employees would call it), or just plain workaholism. Whatever the cause, Dave is the one who sets the pace for the company. He brings in last-minute business on a regular basis and demands that employees work excessive overtime to meet unreasonable deadlines. Despite the experience or expertise of the other financial planners in the company, Dave constantly makes last-minute changes in their reports and proposals.

Like dutiful codependents, Dave's employees scramble to clean up his messes and make his last-minute changes time after time. Dave has never yet had to face a client and say that he could not carry out an unrealistic promise, because his employees always sacrifice themselves to make sure the promise is carried out. Why do Dave's employees protect him and pick up the pieces for him? Perhaps some of them are acting out their experiences as codependents in their family lives. It may seem normal to some of them to function in this manner.

If you are encountering similar cultures, unless you see a real opportunity to change them (which is usually beyond the power of one person), you should consider moving to another company when the opportunity becomes available. If you choose to stay in an abusive situation, realize that your self-esteem may be damaged by the effects of the abuse. It helps to be aware that the abuse is because of the negative culture, rather than a flaw in you, but it is still difficult to weather abuse day in and day out.

Don't Let Yourself Be Too Bound by Your Company's Culture

Though it is politically smart to play by the unwritten rules and acknowledge the real seats of power, you should never let that prevent you from stretching and growing in your job. In other words, don't be afraid to test the limits of corporate culture and traditions. Maybe no one in your position has ever made a proposal to change the system or create a new product before. Remember the story in chapter 5 about the janitor at AlkaSeltzer who suggested a way to increase sales? Don't let culture hold you back from excelling in your job. Who knows? You may start a whole new direction for your company that will benefit you both.

Ethics: A Sticky Subject

Ethics is defined by *The American Heritage Dictionary, Third Edition* as "a set of principles of right conduct." The same dictionary defines a value as "a principle, standard or quality considered worthwhile or desirable." That would seem to say that ethics are principles that people tend to believe are right, as opposed to wrong, whereas a principle held as a value, or considered desirable to one person may not be considered a value to someone else. It seems a fair conclusion to say that peoples' values, or what they consider worthwhile and desirable, will affect their ethics.

Every individual has a set of internal values developed from various influences, including parents, teachers, churches, the media, and personal experience. Professed values, however, sometimes conflict with actual ethical practices. Every organization also has a set of values, which may or may not conflict with its ethical practices. For example, a company may state that it "values" trust in its customer relationships. However, it may use questionable ethics in hiding certain charges in its billing. In such a case, the real value that motivates ethical behavior may be profit.

Probably no individual working for an organization today will agree with every value or ethical practice held by that organization. After all, your values and ethics are motivated by different needs and experiences than those of the company. You may think that it is unethical for your employer to dock you 15 minutes pay if you are 5 minutes late, because you are motivated by your own financial values. But the company is operating from rules that say you are timed in quarter hours, in order to protect its value of employee punctuality. On the other hand, maybe the company only pays you 25 cents a mile for travel when the IRS allows 28 cents a mile.

Such minor differences in values are really not crucial to your comfort level with an organization. You should realize that there may always be some conflicts of this nature. But look at the big picture. What about cutting corners in production, taking responsibility for the quality of products and services, delivering on promises and guarantees? What about social responsibility? Environmental responsibility? In the long run, the company will suffer from ignoring the values of society in its ethical practices. And you may suffer as well if you are closely involved with such practices.

Ethics are becoming an important part of long-range strategic business planning, because it's good business. Many businesses have developed written mission statements to identify their values and ethical practices for their employees. Such statements act as a guide for employees conducting business at all levels of the company. The most effective mission statements are those that have incorporated input from everyone in the company, because they are a fair representation of the values held by all employees. Employees are much more likely to support something they have helped to create.

Here are some suggestions for evaluating the values and ethical practices of your company.

Read the Company's Written Mission Statement

If your company has a written statement, read it and analyze it carefully. What are the values underlying the statement? What does it imply for ethical conduct, particularly in the areas that affect your job? Is the statement clear, or is it vague and ambiguous? Do you notice a discrepancy between the statement and your company's ethical practices?

If you find the statement vague or incongruent with actual practices, ask for some feedback from other employees and your supervisor. You may want to suggest ways the statement could be updated or made to reflect current company values more accurately.

If your company has no mission statement, suggest that it create one. If you feel comfortable doing so, you might suggest writing a draft yourself and letting your company's management review and revise it. Point out that a written statement will enhance the way all employees conduct the company's business. It will guide them to make decisions that affect the company's bottom line in a more efficient manner. Also point out that it will be more difficult for employees to stray from the company's ethical standards if those standards are clearly spelled out in writing.

Compare Your Company's Values to Your Own

If you find significant discrepancies between your values and ethics and your company's, you need to analyze how important these discrepancies are to your job satisfaction. You are the only one who can decide whether you can compromise your personal values. If the discrepancy has to do with a minor issue that relates to the employer's legitimate needs versus your personal needs, it may not be a serious problem. You will always have to compromise somewhat in this area. But a value difference resulting in a serious ethical conflict should be carefully evaluated. You may be jeopardizing your own reputation or career by staying with a company that has a serious ethical problem.

When You Are Unsure about an Ethical Question, Consult Your Supervisor

Rather than make a decision on your own, you should consult with your supervisor if a situation occurs that is not ethically clear. If you make a decision without input from someone higher up in the company, it may turn out to be the wrong decision. Asking for advice from a superior will help protect you from the consequences of a wrong decision.

If You Are Asked to Do Something Unethical, Get Your Boss's Sign-off

There may be times when your boss or your company asks you to do something you do not believe is ethical. If that occurs, always point out your belief that the action is not ethical and that you would prefer not to be involved with it. You should also point out the possible damage to the company's reputation. In order to stand your ground, however, you may risk the perception that you are not a team player. It is up to you to decide what your priority is.

If you are still required to perform an action you believe is unethical, ask your boss to sign off on the action so that you are not held responsible. (Of course, if the action is downright illegal, you are better off to refuse and resign if necessary.) If that kind of thing occurs often, you should consider leaving the company.

You must decide for yourself how you best fit into your company's structure, culture, and ethics. You may have to make some compromises along the way, but following some of the suggestions in this chapter, you should be able to cope with whatever situations you encounter. You may even suggest some improvements to help your company be more prosperous and satisfying for its employees.

To conclude this chapter, here is a story about a company that has done some positive things for itself and its employees. YSI, Inc. in Yellow Springs, Ohio, is a precision laboratory instruments maker. The company was founded by three graduates of Antioch College in 1948. It developed many innovative and successful products such as the first commercial heart-lung machine (1956) and the first instantaneous blood gas analyzer (1957).

By 1985, growth began leveling off. Malte von Matthiessen, an Antioch college graduate and NCR personnel director, took over as president. He is a firm believer in self-management, a system that increases employee participation and rewards employees who help the company grow. Employees now own 55 percent of the company through an employee stock ownership plan (ESOP). YSI also underwent restructuring.

Von Matthiessen cut middle management from five layers to one. He set up self-directed teams of employees who work together and supervise themselves. Managers who doubted the effectiveness of the team concept are now seeing profitable gains for the company. Sales increased 61 percent to $29 million and profits jumped 246 percent to $1.4 million from 1985 to 1990. Earnings per share jumped from $1.90 to $6.29.

The corporate culture of YSI is informal. There are no reserved parking spots. Everyone uses first names, and blue jeans are commonly worn even by the president. There are no time clocks, and employees work on flex-time. No one has been laid off since 1955, and employees have voted to take across-the-board salary cuts and reduce work hours in slow economic times. They even vote on stock option plans for top management. Says von Matthiessen, "Everybody gets their say."[4]

YSI is a living example of treating its employees as it would want to be treated. There are no structural or cultural problems here, and few, if any, ethics problems. It embodies the direction that organizations must take to survive and prosper in the nineties. As Stephen Covey, author of *The Seven Habits of Highly Effective People*, put it, "No matter how much lip service you give to quality, true quality is only born of an organization that's held together by trust and teamwork."[5]

The Stress Cycle: Physical Signs

11

A recent survey of full-time workers conducted for Northwestern National Life Insurance Company concluded that three out of four Americans are stressed-out on their jobs, most to the point of burnout.[1]

Consider findings such as those of Dr. Roy Meninger of the Meninger Foundation, which cite 75 to 80 percent of reported illness as stress-related.[2] The National Institute for Occupational Safety and Health has identified the ten leading work-related health problems as all being related to stress. And a growing number of states' workers' compensation laws are permitting compensation for claims resulting from stress on the job.

Is it any wonder that health insurance ranks as number one in importance to employees? Or that, according to a nationwide survey by the National Federation of Independent Business, businesses all over the country consider the cost of healthcare insurance to be their primary concern?[3]

What Is This Thing Called Stress?

Stress in itself is not bad. It can be positive or negative, stimulating or debilitating. Stress is simply the mental and physical tension that occurs when you do something other than stand, sit, or lie still. No stress at all means you're either asleep, unconscious, or dead! Some stress is necessary and healthy to keep you active and motivated. This chapter will concentrate on the physical aspects of the stress cycle. The mental and emotional aspects will be addressed in the next chapter.

Here's what happens physically when you experience stress: your senses sharpen, your muscles tense, you breathe faster, your heart rate and blood pressure rise, and hormones such as adrenalin and cortisol are released. This occurs in response to positive as well as negative stimuli. But once the stimulus is gone, or you resolve or accept the stressful situation, the stress passes and the physical symptoms subside—or do they?

If you operate under chronic stress, even relatively positive stress such as overworking yourself on a job you enjoy, your body is not allowed to relax and return to its less energized state long enough to recover from the effects. Your muscles contract without release, blood vessels constrict, and blood flow decreases. Your muscles become starved for oxygen and signal their distress with pain.

Warning Signs: The Most Common Physical Symptoms

Do you experience a lot of headaches? Is neck, shoulder, or back pain a common occurrence for you? Have you noticed more indigestion and even frequent stomach pain? You might even be wondering why you seem to get so many colds or sinus infections. They are all common symptoms of unrelieved or improperly handled stress. The more severe and prolonged cases can result in ulcers, high blood pressure, heart disease, and arthritis.

Because chronic and severe stress tends to attack whatever part of your body is most vulnerable, the symptoms will vary with each individual. Therefore, whatever inherited tendencies or other physical risks you may have will be aggravated by stress. That includes addictive patterns such as drug and alcohol abuse. Though addictions have a strong physical component, their source is primarily mental or emotional, so they will be discussed in the next chapter.

Why Are We So Vulnerable to Stress Today?

Recall from chapter 1 that our nation is in the throes of the technological revolution. Dealing with this kind of change and pressure creates a lot of stress for anyone, but it has become even greater for our present generation. Never has so much change occurred so fast and with so little preparation. Remember that the industrial revolution took from 100 to 150 years to bring about the kinds of changes we have seen in the last 30 years.

The Baby Boomer generation (born 1946–1964) is more vulnerable to stress than previous generations because we have fewer support systems. Radical lifestyle changes have eliminated the predominance of early marriages, large families, religion, and stability. Whereas most Baby Boomers' fathers worked for the same organization for 30 or 40 years, now mothers and fathers are changing jobs an average of three or four times during their work life. Divorce and remarriage is much more prevalent, resulting in more single-parent households and whole new family structures. Children may get new parents, and parents "new" children, almost as often as parents get new jobs. Without the stability and traditional methods of support, the Baby Boomers, and the following generation of Baby Busters (born 1965–1973), are suffering even greater effects of stress.

Organizations Are Recognizing the Need for Stress Management

Because of the skyrocketing cost of healthcare and the many links between health problems and stress, many companies are implementing stress management programs. Most larger companies have some form of employee assistance or wellness program, and many smaller organizations are following suit. These businesses are beginning to realize that prevention is often much more cost-efficient than necessary cures. For example, many are realizing that it makes sense to pay for an addiction recovery program before an addicted employee gets to the stage of needing serious physical treatment or surgery. It also makes sense to promote stress-relieving fitness programs, rather than waiting for an overworked, overstressed employee to need a $30,000 heart bypass operation.

If your company has a wellness or employee assistance program, here is the kind of help you may be able to get:

- Literature should be available that states how the program operates with a clearly stated policy describing how the company will help with particular problems or needs.

- Often a short-term counseling service is available during off-hours at no charge to the employee. This may be a twenty-four-hour help line or a contracted service that you can visit locally.
- Some type of fitness or wellness program is usually included with exercise or aerobics classes, free or reduced-cost use of health club facilities, or an incentive program that rewards you for fitness activities you do on your own.

Don't hesitate to take advantage of such a program if it is available to you. If your organization does not have such a program, you may want to propose that the possibility be investigated. Chapter 15 will provide you with some information about the cost benefits for your company that you can show to your management people.

How You Can Recognize Your Stress Level

Stress usually begins with a feeling of being challenged or threatened. Your brain signals to certain glands, which in turn send out chemical signals, and stress hormones pour into your bloodstream. You feel the effects immediately. Your heart rate goes up, your blood pressure increases, your pupils dilate, your blood volume and sodium levels increase and more blood is directed to your muscles and liver for quick energy. Normally, after the threat is over, your body automatically reverses the stress reaction and returns to normal. But if you are exposed to stress repeatedly, or if it continues without a break for long periods of time, your body can no longer recover from the stress response and you begin to experience physical symptoms such as headaches, backaches, and so on.

As mentioned earlier, headaches, backaches, stomach problems, and over-susceptibility to colds and sinus infections are common warning signs that your stress level is too high. However, many people do not realize that those symptoms are due to stress. Of course, they can be symptoms of some other physical ailment, but all too often they are telling you that there is too much unrelieved stress in your life. Take the following quiz to see if your body is trying to tell you something.

Are you experiencing:

	Frequently	Occasionally	Rarely/Never
1. Head, neck, or back aches	3	2	1
2. Fatigue or exhaustion	3	2	1
3. Lack of stamina	3	2	1
4. Poor short-term memory	3	2	1
5. Chest pains or shortness of breath	3	2	1
6. Anxiety or irritability	3	2	1
7. Indigestion or stomach pains	3	2	1
8. Difficulty sleeping	3	2	1
9. Inability to relax	3	2	1
10. Rushed or skipped meals	3	2	1
11. Little or no exercise	3	2	1
12. Increase or decrease in appetite	3	2	1
13. Increased mistakes or accidents	3	2	1

Scoring: A score of 15 or lower indicates you have a low degree of stress in your life; 16-26 means you have an average amount of stress; 27 or higher means your stress level is particularly high.

This test is intended not as a scientific diagnosis but merely as a guide to the level of stress you are currently experiencing. Knowing your own personality and physical condition will help you determine how much stress you can manage adequately before you decide you need professional help.

Different Personality Types Can Handle Different Stress Levels

You have probably heard of Type A and Type B personalities. Type As correspond to the people-person and command-person types. These outgoing, dynamic, energetic types can handle a somewhat higher stress level than the calmer, more introverted Type Bs, who correspond to the detail-person and support-person types. In fact, Type As are often aggressive, competitive workaholics, many of whom are candidates for heart attacks. On the other hand, Type Bs may tend to be cautious hypochondriacs and tend to hold more negative feelings inside where they can do as much damage as explosive outbursts.

These are only tendencies, of course, and they will be affected by an individual's heredity and current physical condition. They may help you understand why you are able or unable to tolerate certain levels and kinds of stress.

How You Can Cope with Your Stress Level

Medical research shows that exercising and being aerobically fit can temper the effects of stress and make it easier to handle. Conditioning limits the rise in stress hormones and therefore limits the amount your heart rate will jump during stress. Quick jumps in heart rate have been linked to heart attacks, particularly for Type A personalities, so being in good condition can actually save your life. Because a fit body doesn't release as much stress hormone into your system, your body can also return to normal more quickly after a stress response.

Regular physical exercise also releases endorphins into your system. Endorphins are a biochemical that give you a natural high, which is what runners often experience. This chemical makes you feel good, helps to stabilize the effect of stress hormones, and minimizes pain. To get the maximum benefit from endorphins, it is necessary to exercise regularly. There is a point of overdoing, however. Above a certain intensity, exercise stimulates the same mechanism as stress, and high levels of cortisol can be permanently activated. Chronically elevated levels of cortisol can cause suppression of the immune systems, depression, and other serious problems.

Type A personalities sometimes become actual stress addicts. They can't stop their harried lifestyles because they are hooked on the rush of adrenalin they get from their body's stress response. Though some Type As may enjoy this kind of behavior, they are not doing their bodies any favors, nor their Type B coworkers whose stress is being increased by their demands.

One interesting method of coping with stress is to cry. It has been found that tears contain high levels of stress hormones. Crying appears to be one way of releasing excess hormones from the body. Women, on the whole, tend to suffer from stress less than men do, though that is changing in today's work force. The greater societal acceptance of women's crying may play a big part in helping them cope with stress.

Some methods of coping with stress, such as smoking, drinking alcohol or caffeine, and eating foods high in sugar, salt, or fat, actually increase stress, rather than relieve it. Skipping meals and sacrificing sleep also aggravate and add to stressful conditions. Keeping yourself in the best possible physical condition will help reduce the effects of your body's stress response and lessen the physical damage excessive or chronic stress can cause.

Your attitude plays a large role in how effective exercise is in keeping you in shape and lowering your stress level. If you exercise primarily because you think you should, you'll probably add more stress to your life. Try to find some type of exercise you enjoy doing. Whether you choose to play a competitive sport, walk with your spouse or a friend, dance to rock music, or romp in the backyard or park with your kids, make it a fun part of your life and it will prove to be much more beneficial.

Regarding sleep, not everyone needs eight hours, but no one can function properly on two or three either. In an emergency you may be able to get away with a couple of hours of sleep, but attempting to do that on a regular basis will not prepare you to handle either good or bad stress. Some Type A people think sleep is a waste of time, but eventually they will feel the consequences in increased physical symptoms of high stress.

Diet is also very important to controlling stress. Excessive sugar, salt, fat, and caffeine have helped to put one out of every two Americans at risk for coronary heart disease. Heart disease is still the number one killer in the United States, and coronary bypass surgery claims more healthcare dollars than any other operation, costing more than $5 billion annually. That has led to concern about lowering cholesterol, as well as sugar, among food manufacturers and restaurants.

"Sugar-free" and "cholesterol-free" are showing up on numerous signs and labels. "Sugar-free" usually means an artificial sweetener is used, which may cause other health problems in some people. Also, "sugar-free" does not mean calorie-free. Products labeled "cholesterol-free," such as salad dressing or margarine, may still be dripping with saturated fat. Saturated fat actually boosts the cholesterol manufactured by your own body. "Fat-free" products are also on the market, but fat-free does not mean calorie-free either.

A diet rich in complex carbohydrates, such as whole grain cereals, breads, and pasta, combined with protein and dairy products, which slow down sugar absorption, will give you the steady energy supply you need. Your diet can play a crucial role in stress management. Eat when you are relaxed; a rushed meal under pressure can raise blood cholesterol by as much as 50 percent. And don't skip any meals. That slows your metabolism and causes your body to store more fat.

Some Quick and Easy Physical Stress Reducers

If you work in an office, you undoubtedly sit too much and move too little. Try some exercises that gently stretch your muscles to keep you limber, relieve tension, and prevent knots and spasms. This type of exercise is a good complement to brisk walking, bicycling, or other aerobic exercises, and you can do it almost anywhere, anytime.

Deep Breathing Control

Stress creates rapid breathing, so slowing down your breathing can help control the stress response. It also cuts down adrenalin and cortisol flow during periods of stress. Remember the advice about taking a deep breath and counting to ten when you're upset? It works!

Try the 6–3–6 method of deep breathing control suggested by the Chicago School of Massage Therapy. Inhale for a count of six. Hold that breath for a count of three. Then exhale for a count of six. Breathe through your nose instead of your mouth as that also slows breathing. Be sure to breathe deeply from the diaphragm, which is the muscle that separates your chest from your abdomen.

Progressive Muscle Relaxation

Alternately tense and relax sets of muscles while sitting at your desk. Start with the toes, and slowly work all the way up to the forehead. Your face and jaw muscles can become extremely tense under stress. Breathe regularly for about 20 seconds. Repeat the process a couple of times until you feel relaxed. It may also help you visualize some soothing imagery while doing this. Imagine yourself lying on a beach or floating in a pool. Progressive muscle relaxation will increase your awareness of your body and let you know what weak points absorb the most tension.

You can do a quick version of progressive relaxation. Sit or lie down, or lean against something while standing. Inhale and hold for a count of six while tensing as many muscles as you can. Then exhale quickly and let your body go limp, breathing regularly. You can repeat this a couple of times until you feel fully relaxed, breathing regularly in-between each time.

Take a Walk

Another quick way to relieve stress is to take a ten-minute walk. A brisk ten-minute walk can decrease tension and stress for up to one hour afterward. It will calm you down but also leave you feeling energized. Getting away from a problem always helps to clear your mind and give you a fresh outlook.

Some More Advanced Stress Reducers

These are some advanced techniques that can be helpful. If you suffer from severe or chronic stress, you may want to investigate them.

Massage Therapy

Massage therapy includes a number of techniques, such as the relaxing Swedish massage and stimulating Shiatsu. Though you may enjoy doing this with members of your family, a licensed massage therapist can give you the professional treatment that's right for your needs and physical condition.

Self-help Groups

Self-help groups are being created everywhere to help you cope with everything from alcoholism to obesity to caring for your elderly parents. You may find that a group helps you cope with stress in general or helps you deal with any specific problem you may be having.

Meditation

Meditation combines movement, breathing techniques, sensory awareness, and positive imagery. Many classes are available on all types of meditation, and the techniques you learn can be used anytime, at home or at work. Even good, old-fashioned prayer, or devotional time, is a form of meditation that can be extremely effective for reducing the physical as well as mental effects of stress.

A Word about Ergonomics

One of the major causes of physical stress and, subsequently, the second most frequently performed surgery in the United States, is an improperly designed workstation. Since the advent of the computer age, the rate of occurrence of cumulative trauma disorders, or repetitive stress injuries, has tripled.

Repetitive stress injuries, which now account for 56 percent of all work-related illnesses, is the collective name for injuries caused by repeated motions, pressure, or vibrations over a long period of time.[4] This includes problems such as tennis elbow, tendinitis, fibrositis and, the most common, carpal tunnel syndrome. Carpal tunnel syndrome now results in the second most frequently performed surgery in the nation. In 1990 alone, worker's compensation and absenteeism cost U.S. employers more than $20 billion.[5]

If your job involves repetitive or forceful hand movements, such as operating a keyboard or other automated equipment operation, you may have already experienced painful tingling, weakness, or numbness in one or both hands. Repetitive motion causes the tissues surrounding the bones at the base of the wrist to become inflamed and swollen. The swelling pinches or compresses the median nerve that runs through this carpal tunnel area in the wrist. Continued movement, without adequate recovery time to let the inflammation subside, can result in serious pain and numbness that can only be relieved by surgery. Left untreated, problems may even spread to the back, shoulders, and neck. However, carpal tunnel syndrome can be prevented and even reversed before surgery becomes necessary.

Lower back problems are another major result of the physical stress of modern work environments. A chair that doesn't give proper support or is too large or small for the worker, improper lifting, and lifting items that are too heavy are some causes of back injuries. The United States currently spends more than $30 billion annually on worker compensation for lower back injuries, up from $14 billion less than ten years ago.

The causes of repetitive stress injuries and back injuries are linked to job design factors which have formed a new science called ergonomics. Ergonomics is the study of how people interact with their physical environment and why certain injuries occur when specific tasks are performed. The U.S. National Institute of Occupational Health and Safety found that proper ergonomic design leads to a 24.7 percent increase in productivity among workers.

Here are some suggestions on how to relieve workstation stress and prevent injuries requiring serious medical treatment.

- Tailor the computer or workstation to the user, not the other way around. Carpal tunnel irritation occurs most readily when the wrists are bent at an angle. To prevent that, never place a computer on a standard 29-inch-high desk. The keyboard should be placed at a level about 26 inches from the floor, the height of a standard typewriter table. Adjustable chairs and variable height keyboard stands will compensate for individual height and comfort.
- A job rotation system that allows performance of other tasks at various times of the day will help relieve long-term irritation and stress. Continuous keyboard operation should be relieved by a work/rest cycle, allowing breaks approximately every 30 minutes.
- If you already suffer from carpal tunnel syndrome or lower back problems, all of the above will help reverse the effects, but you should also see your doctor. He or she may prescribe medication that can relieve symptoms before surgery becomes necessary.

If any of the above suggestions require major changes in your work environment, don't be reluctant to bring them to the attention of your boss. Point out the possibility of expensive medical care that may be needed if you do not get relief from these problems. A change in workstation equipment will certainly cost less in the long run than medical treatment, surgery, lost productivity, and sick leave.

The Cost of Stress

Whatever suggestions you find for reducing stress and its physical consequences, either in this book, or on your own, should be eagerly supported by your employer. Point out the benefits of promoting fitness and other stress reduction activities in terms of increased productivity, lowered healthcare costs, and higher morale.

Your employer should be happy to let you start an after-work aerobics group or teach deep breathing control techniques on your lunch hour. As long as you don't interfere with the regular work routine, any activity that encourages your coworkers to manage stress can only benefit your employer and your company.

The next chapter talks about the mental and emotional aspects of stress and the consequences of improper coping or not coping at all. You will learn techniques to cope with emotional symptoms that can result in physical illness and help prevent such severe emotional problems as depression and burnout. So take a deep breath and keep reading!

The Stress Cycle: Mental/Emotional Signs 12

Remember the last time your boss snarled that you should have known about something in a report you never even received? It follows that if his physical senses are heightened and adrenalin flow is increased under stress, then his mental processes are also working faster than normal. In fact, long after the physical symptoms of stress have ceased, he may still be experiencing the mental and emotional symptoms of stress such as worry, anxiety, anger, and depression. Such symptoms can spill out in unexpected outbursts like the one from your boss.

If something upsetting occurs at work, do you continue to mull over the future consequences of the incident after you get home? Do you worry that it might happen again? Do you feel anxious about what the implications may be for you and your job? Do you get downright angry that whatever happened may jeopardize your position or job? Or do you let yourself slide into a depression because you think you have no control over the matter? All of those responses are the mental and emotional symptoms of stress. Your response may depend on your personality type and your individual level of experience and maturity. The most important thing to remember is that how you cope with these responses will determine how seriously they will affect you, your job performance, and your life.

The Japanese offer an example of a society where stress responses are out of control. They are a society of overachievers, and no one would doubt their success in the world marketplace. But what has been the price of that success? Japanese executives are driven to produce and are devastated by failure. They are consumed by guilt, even for taking time off for a holiday or illness. Most Japanese work a 72-hour workweek, and few take their allotted vacation time for fear of losing favor with their bosses. Job-related stress has produced an alarming increase in alcoholism, mental breakdowns, suicides, and family abandonment in the last decade.

That is a case where a nation has a system of overwhelming stress but no appropriate way to cope with it. Expectations of continually high performance and production levels without adequate relief have led Japanese workers to express major dissatisfaction with the system, which is surprising in light of the Japanese philosophy of accepting sacrifice and foregoing personal well-being for the good of the country. Polls comparing American and Japanese feelings about their lives consistently show that the Japanese are far less satisfied with their family life, leisure time, and general quality of life than Americans.[1]

Though Americans may have a better balance of work, family, and leisure time, we are not coping with stress much better than the Japanese. Alcohol and drug abuse cost the United States more than $100 billion a year in increased medical expenses, workers' compensation claims, lost time, and productivity. Using alcohol and drugs to cope with the mental and emotional effects of stress is costly and damaging. In this chapter we will examine the types of mental and emotional responses to stress and healthy, effective ways to cope with them.

How Does Your Personality Handle Mental and Emotional Stress?

Type A personalities are generally optimistic and resilient, not allowing setbacks to slow them down. They can usually handle a lot of stress and pressure without falling apart. They actually seem to thrive on pressure, but they also tend to be hot reactors. They tend to fly off the handle and openly express their impatience, displeasure, and anger. Because they are ambitious go-getters, they often put in long hours and ignore their physical needs and limitations, as well as their emotional capability to handle stress. You might say Type As think they are invulnerable, or at least they behave as if they do.

In comparison, Type Bs, the equivalent of detail-persons and support-persons, tend to be cautious and methodical in their approach to tasks. They tend to be more easily discouraged by setbacks or at least react more slowly and carefully the next time they try a project. They are more reluctant to express their feelings and tend to hold resentment or anger inside. Holding such feelings inside can actually make them candidates for physical illness. The emotional pressure has to come out somewhere, and it will likely attack the most vulnerable physical area of the Type B person. Type Bs are usually more likely to balk at pressure, but they are more thorough, patient, and perfectionistic than the Type A who wants to get results quickly. For this reason, Type B people often suffer high stress and anxiety when they are not given enough time to accomplish a task properly.

All of these tendencies will be affected by your individuality. You may even be a combination of the two types, though one is probably dominant in you. As a generality though, Type As are concerned with quantity whereas Type Bs are more concerned with quality. That may just be because Type As expect their efforts to be quality because of their natural self-confidence and optimism. Being more pessimistic, Type Bs worry more about accomplishing the quality, taking time to make sure every detail is perfect. It can be helpful to recognize these tendencies in yourself and your coworkers, especially when you must deal with the stress they cause.

Understanding your stress response is the key to changing it. You can learn to rethink old emotional habits. Think through the alternatives at hand and find a way to make the best of the circumstances. That sounds simplistic, but does it make more sense to fly off the handle or suffer in silence? This attitude toward stress is summed up in a famous prayer known as the Serenity Prayer: "God, grant me the grace to accept with serenity the things I cannot change, the courage to change the things I can, and the wisdom to know the difference."

What Can Happen When Mental or Emotional Stress Is Not Properly Managed?

An overload of stress usually shows up in symptoms such as chronic fatigue, withdrawal from coworkers, family and friends, decline in work performance, and an increased need for escape activities. Those symptoms can also be a sign of a much more severe reaction to stress overload called "burnout." Whereas stressed-out people may be *too* involved with their work, burned-out people no longer feel involved with theirs. According to psychologists, burnout occurs when the pressures and conflicts outnumber the emotional rewards of a job. Working under highly stressful conditions too long without adequate coping methods or relief can create a feeling of being out of control and without purpose, or a sense of futility. In other words, you give up.

Burnout is also the result of unrealistic expectations, imposed either by the employee, a boss, or a company. Herbert J. Freudenberger, a New York psychologist and author of *Burnout: How to Beat the High Cost of Success*, says there is a wearing down of hopes and ideals as employees strive to reach some unrealistic expectation.

Bosses who constantly point out problems in employees' work, without giving praise for accomplishments, are setting their employees up for eventual burnout. The feelings of helplessness and hopelessness kill motivation. That is where burnout differs from stress. People who are simply stressed out can still be highly motivated. Burned-out employees will usually either leave or become physically or emotionally ill.

Freudenberger describes employees who are burning out: "Their self-control snaps, and all their pent-up resentments burst forth in displays that are completely out of character but reveal classic burnout reactions: cynicism, heightened irritability, mistrust of others, paranoia, and grandiosity."[2]

Another serious consequence of unmanaged, unrelenting stress is depression. A person may go through a cycle that begins with symptoms of excessive stress, then progresses to eventual burnout, and, finally, becomes a serious depression. Or, a person may slip into depression at the first signs of excessive stress. It depends on the individual's personality, outlook on life, physical condition, and demands from other areas of his or her life.

Almost everyone gets the blues or has short periods of depression. It is normal to experience depression following a distressing event or loss. But when depression persists for weeks or months, interfering with relationships, family life, work, or even physical health, it may be what psychologists call clinical depression. This kind of depression is caused by a depletion of biochemicals in the brain. The condition exhibits many of the symptoms of excessive stress and burnout such as irritability, fatigue, headaches, backaches, digestive problems, and a feeling of hopelessness. You may also notice sleep and appetite disturbances and emotional instability which can include crying spells.

Clinical depression requires professional counseling and treatment. As many as 15 million Americans may be experiencing clinical depression without realizing it. Because it is such a common ailment, most people don't recognize it or they try to ignore it. Left untreated, depression can lead to significant health problems.

Are You at Risk for Burnout or Depression?

This brief test will help you determine whether or not you are currently at risk for burnout or serious depression. It is not intended as a diagnosis of either condition. Your score can serve as a warning. You may decide to seek professional counseling to determine the extent of your need.

In the last two weeks, have you been:

	Frequently	Occasionally	Rarely/ Never
1. Uninterested in things you used to enjoy	3	2	1
2. Experiencing wide mood swings	3	2	1
3. Feeling irritable and anxious	3	2	1
4. Feeling your life is out of control	3	2	1
5. Overwhelmed by everyday affairs and trivial problems	3	2	1
6. Feeling useless and unneeded	3	2	1
7. Having difficulty sleeping	3	2	1
8. Noticing a decrease (or increase) in your appetite	3	2	1
9. Feeling tired with little energy for no apparent reason	3	2	1
10. Experiencing unexplained physical ailments (headaches, backaches, stomach upsets, rapid heartbeat)	3	2	1

Total Score _____

Scoring: below 15 = low risk; 15-20 = moderate risk; Over 20 = high risk

First Aid for Mental or Emotional Stress

The following is a list of ten specific ways to manage and cope with the stress you face. These suggestions will not cure all of your stress-related problems, but they will certainly help you manage stress in a more positive way. Furthermore, these techniques can help prevent some of the serious problems that might occur if you are unable to cope with stress in your life. Think of these ideas as first aid for stress.

1. Monitor Your Stress Patterns

What are the specific causes of stress in your life, and how are they affecting you? How are you responding? A good way to keep track is to write it down. Keep a journal or notebook for a couple of weeks, noting when stressful events happen, who or what they involve, and how you respond. You will begin to see a pattern. You will recognize what specific tasks or people seem to put you in a stressful situation on a regular basis. Remember to include positive stress too. Even events such as a wedding or Christmas can add to your overall stress level.

This analysis can help you become more aware of the things you can change and the things you can't. The things you can't alter require a change in your response to them. Writing down your thoughts and feelings when a stressful event occurs gives you a chance to reflect on them later and to determine the best way to handle the event. Don't lay awake at night, losing healthy sleep mulling over problems you can think about at a more appropriate time. Scarlett O'Hara had the right idea when she said, "I'll think about it tomorrow." On the other hand, you don't want to procrastinate on things you can do something about, because that only prolongs the stress.

2. Work on Your Attitude

Once you've determined the kind of stress you are experiencing and how you will deal with it, start working on your stress response. For example, you may want to rethink your emotional habits of flying off the handle or keeping all your feelings inside. Neither of those reactions is productive. Saying the Serenity Prayer is an excellent way to achieve balance with your reactions.

Remember the negative programming from chapter 3? If you anticipate problems based on what your programming tells you, you may actually create them. Before a stressful event, picture yourself doing well, handling it with confidence. During the event, don't listen to the negative tapes playing in your head. For example, if you are nervous about speaking to a group of people, your tapes might be saying, "They're not listening. They think you don't know what you're talking about." Override such thoughts with rational ones that say, "Keep going. You don't know what they really think. They may be annoyed because the room's too cold, but they're really interested in what you're saying." If you think you're falling apart, you eventually will. The trick is to tell yourself you're not going to fall apart and you won't.

After the event, don't criticize yourself. Maybe you did make a couple of mistakes. That's OK. Make a note to correct them the next time, but concentrate on what you did well and what you're going to do next. If you learn to control your anxiety this way, each time you face a stressful event you will be more in control and actually reduce your stress.

Another important attitude about stress is thinking of it as temporary. You may be in the middle of a situation or period right now that seems like a killer, but will it be over soon? Look at one of your old datebooks or calendars. Look at some of the stressful events or periods of your life you have already come through. They seemed like all-consuming crises at the time, but you've probably forgotten them by now. It does help to remember that temporary stress will eventually be over. You can look forward to putting it all behind you and rewarding yourself with some well-deserved relaxation.

3. Take Responsibility for Your Own Successes and Failures

Realize that your successes and failures are important life lessons. You should learn as much from your mistakes as you do from your triumphs. Be patient with yourself as you learn, grow, and change. Taking this attitude with yourself and others can have a major impact on reducing your stress.

4. Balance Your Work and Personal Life

You should never be so emotionally tied to your job that you have no outside interests. Particularly in today's economy, when job loss is so prevalent, you are setting yourself up for emotional disaster.

If you are male, you know that the first question people ask when they meet you is, "What do you do for a living?" In our culture, men have their worth defined by their work. It is important to remember, however, that you are much more than your job. It is only one part of your life. It is also important to remember your priorities. Try to give your family, friends, hobbies, and recreation at least as much time as you do your job.

A Gallup poll found that women who were satisfied with their jobs were also likely to be happy with their family life. Most of those who weren't satisfied with their jobs weren't satisfied with their family life either. That's an interesting correlation in light of the myth that a satisfying career was a threat to a happy family life for a woman.

5. Get Support

You need your family, friends, and coworkers for emotional support and constructive, caring feedback. It is always easier when you don't have to face things alone. Talking with someone who cares about you can alleviate a lot of stress and worry. You also need at least one confidant who will be honest and fairly objective. A person who merely commiserates with you or criticizes too much will not be helpful.

You should never hesitate to seek help from all available resources, such as your employee assistance program, self-help groups, or professional counseling. The smartest thing you can do is to get help with a problem before it becomes overwhelming.

6. Take a New Look at What You Think Is Expected of You

You were programmed at an early age with messages about what you should or should not be. That programming has added to your stress. Our society tells you that you must be perfect, fast, strong, and say yes. In other words, don't make mistakes, get it done immediately, don't show any weakness, and always do what others ask of you. Is that realistic? Is any of us superman or superwoman? No, we're vulnerable human beings. On the job, the golden rule might be, "I won't make unreasonable demands of you, if you don't make unreasonable demands of me." Try the same approach with yourself: treat yourself as you would want others to treat you. Know your limitations, accept them, and set boundaries accordingly.

7. Make Large Tasks More Manageable by Dividing Them into Smaller Tasks

When you have a large project to tackle, the stress of facing it can make it more difficult than it has to be. Break it down into smaller tasks, starting with the easiest parts first, so you feel like you're making headway. If at all possible, take a break before going on to the next task. Make sure you have realistic deadlines, or ask for help if you need it. Remember the adage "Do you want it Tuesday, or do you want it right?"

It also helps to organize the tasks in such a way that you are most productive. For example, if you have to check something in another department, save that part of the task until you are going to that area anyway. Or, make sure you handle time-sensitive tasks right away. Don't waste time struggling with something that requires help. Move on to another part of the project and put that task off until you can get appropriate help. Any way you can save time and effort for yourself will also reduce your stress.

Here is a special note for those of you who tend to put off projects until the night before they're due. You may think the stress and pressure help you to get the work done, but they could also kill an elephant!

8. Inject Some Humor into Your Work Life

No one can work continuously for eight solid hours (although some bosses would like you to think otherwise). Take a little time to laugh. Laughing is actually good for you physically, and it is one of the greatest emotional stress relievers known to humankind. In fact, humor has been so successful as a stress reducer that it has spawned a whole new breed of stress consultants. John Cleese, of *Monty Python* and

A Fish Called Wanda fame, and many others, use humor therapy in their professional stress relief programs.

9. Take Time for Yourself

Here are some ways to use time creatively to help reduce stress. If you have been working on a problem and can't seem to get anywhere with it, take time out to do something else. Work on something simpler, read a magazine, make a phone call, get a drink of water (not coffee or cola with caffeine). Getting your mind off the problem eases the stress of concentrating too hard on one thing. It allows you to relax a little and lets your thought processes refresh themselves. You can return to it with a new perspective. Psychological studies show that creative ideas occur most easily when you let go of problems and indulge in something pleasurable.

You should also allow yourself some empty time once in a while. Take a mental break and let your mind wander. You might even accidentally wander into a new, creative idea. Planning regular quiet time to think things through and prioritize your goals is good for you.

Learn what your concentration tolerance is during a workday. In other words, how long can you work continuously and still be productive? If you tend to taper off around 3:00 P.M., schedule your simplest non-thinking tasks after 3:00 P.M. Set your watch to beep and remind you when it's time to take a break!

If possible, allow some time to unwind at lunch and when you get home from work. When you get home at night you should completely forget about work. Even if you bring work home, give yourself time to unwind and relax before doing it.

When unwinding, do something completely different from your work. Have fun with your children. Talk with your spouse, preferably not about work. Save that for later. Walk your dog or play chase with your cat. Watch a funny or relaxing TV show—not the news. Rent a movie, or tape your favorite soap opera during the day and watch it when you get home. Go out to dinner, or if you must cook, have fun with it. Try something different and creative.

Become involved with something that makes no or little demands on you for a few hours everyday after work. Deal with family or other problems after you have unwound. You'll have a better attitude and fresher approach once you've unloaded the stress of the day. Even good stress from a job you enjoy needs to be unloaded.

10. Go with the Flow

That may sound like a tired cliche, but in today's economic situation, accepting change can be the most important way to keep stress from getting out of control. It is inevitable that there will be changes in your job, in your organization, even in your career field. If you fear change, it will only add more negative stress to your already stressful life. Of course it is only natural for human beings to fear change and worry about the future. But if you learn to look for the possibilities in change, instead of the problems, you will find that you don't have as much to fear as you thought you did.

Sharon had been doing the same job for fifteen years. She continued to grow and develop in her job as an administrative assistant in an insurance office, learning more about the industry all the time. She felt secure in her position, performing her familiar duties. She had become so knowledgeable about the company's clients and their needs that one day her boss decided he wanted her to step into a different role. He wasn't sure what the position would be, but he knew Sharon's valuable knowledge and ability could help the company identify and service new clients.

The idea was frightening to Sharon at first. Her boss was asking her to take on a new position that wasn't even defined! He could only tell her about a few of the ideas he had for using her expertise to expand the company's market. She began to be overwhelmed by stress as she feared that an ill-defined job function would lead to her failure and loss of a secure career. She continued to protest the change for a while, but her boss insisted that he wanted her to take the step.

Gradually Sharon began to think about the possibilities for her new position. Her boss's confidence in her abilities encouraged her. Eventually Sharon created her own title of marketing specialist and used her boss's ideas as a foundation for designing a whole new marketing program for the company. She experienced a new excitement about her job and found that she was more in control of her career than she had ever been.

Resisting change only increases stress. When you go with the flow, you will still have stress, but coping with it will be much less difficult because your attitude won't be magnifying it. Keeping your mind and emotions open to new possibilities and keeping your body in good physical condition are the most positive steps you can take toward reducing the effects of stress in your life. As one old saying points out, "When life gives you lemons, make lemonade." That's a cute way of saying that you can decide to turn disadvantages into advantages if you're willing to try.

The next chapter will give you some suggestions on how to do just that with two of the most difficult situations in the workplace: dealing with anger and handling criticism.

Handling the Two Bad Words: *Anger* and *Criticism*

13

Without a doubt, anger and criticism can be major contributors to hating your job. Anger toward a coworker, employer, or situation can burn with a destructive intensity. Criticism can chip away at confidence, leaving an almost overwhelming sense of defeat in its wake.

Terry, a systems analyst at a large Midwestern university, creates that sense of defeat in his coworkers. He points out, with discouraging consistency, things his coworkers and even his boss aren't doing right. His approach represents criticism at its worst—it is both insulting and embarrassing to his colleagues.

Victoria, an accountant at a small medical supplies firm, struggles almost daily with the anger she feels about her work environment. "The left hand never knows what the right hand is doing," is the way she characterizes the lack of structure and organization at her firm. When she submits suggestions to improve the company to her employer, she generally receives no response, which only angers her more.

Those are only two examples of the corrosive effect anger and criticism can have on a job. Although anger and criticism in and of themselves are not bad, if they are not handled well, they can have a negative impact on job performance and morale. Let's examine further these two common, but not always well-managed, facets of the job.

Anger: The Misunderstood Emotion

Anger is one of the most common emotions human beings face, especially in the work world. But it is also one of the most misunderstood emotions. Sometimes it is inappropriately dealt with at work or ignored altogether.

First realize that feeling anger is OK. You may be hearing some of those old programming tapes from your childhood that told you anger was bad. If you were punished or ignored for expressing anger, you probably have a difficult time dealing with it now.

But there is nothing wrong with *feeling* anger. It is a feeling like any other feeling and is not wrong in itself. There are even good reasons for feeling anger. You get angry about an injustice, a setback, or a tragedy. The problem can be your response.

You can probably think of an instance where it is not all right to express your anger. Most of us tend to want to repress it, depending on our temperament, the more vocal command-persons and people-persons will more readily express anger, but even they can be controlled by childhood programming. Can you think of an instance when you feel OK about expressing anger?

If you answered no, consider this: Do you ever have a problem controlling your expression of anger? If you said yes, you probably know that this is a double whammy. You believe it's wrong to get angry, yet you have a hard time not getting angry! How does that add up? You'll have major stress. The best way to avoid being stressed-out by this emotion is to decide that it is OK to feel anger. But when is it all right to express it, and how should it be expressed?

There are basically two ways to express anger: outward and inward expressions. The outward expression may be manifested in rage or explosions. The inward expression may show up as resentment and bitterness. The outward expression demonstrates itself directly to the object of the anger, such as yelling at a person or kicking a desk. The inward expression cannot be shown directly to the object of the anger, for whatever reason, so it turns on the angry person and is stuffed inside. Both of these responses create stress and can result in stress-related illnesses such as heart disease and ulcers.

You need to feel your anger, but neither of the above responses is the best way to express it. There is a constructive way to use anger as a motivating force, and it can be outward or inward. If a coworker has done something that you specifically asked him not to do and he has destroyed a project you were both working on, you have a right to be angry. But will it help either of you if you go to him and fly into a rage, provoking his defensive anger as well? Will it help if you don't say anything and stuff your anger inside? Usually stuffed anger builds into full-fledged resentment that damages your ability to work with others.

Have you ever been in the middle of a temper tantrum when the phone rang, or an important person walked into the room? What happened to your anger? You suddenly put it on hold and your behavior immediately changed. But when you hung up or the person left, you went on with your tantrum. If you choose, you can control your emotional response to anger.

What about the coworker who messed up your project? You need to confront the person and let him know that you are angry. You asked him to perform the task a certain way for a reason, and the fact that the project is now in ruins proves your point. He should learn from the mistake he has made, and you are the person who can teach him. Open confrontation is a valid approach, provided you are not patronizing. Remember, someday the shoe could be on the other foot, and that person may be confronting you.

Your anger will propel you to say something to your errant co-worker. Don't be afraid to say something constructive. Let your anger inspire you to say, "Yes, I have a valid reason to correct this person." Then approach him when you are calm, controlled, and rational. Explain the error, the consequences, and the solution. Further explain how you can work together to straighten out the problem. You can help dissipate the tension by remaining calm and in control. This approach practically guarantees good results. You will be able to maintain a good relationship with the coworker and probably salvage the project too. Both of you will feel better about the incident, and it could even strengthen your working relationship.

Let's turn the tables around. Suppose you are on the receiving end of someone's anger. What is the best way to respond? If a colleague or boss is screaming at you, you will not help anything by screaming back—even if you feel justified. First, you need to show that you accept the person's feelings and are willing to *try to understand* what he or she is communicating to you. In other words, "Yes, I see that you are angry, and I'm willing to find out if I've done something to warrant your anger and try to fix it if I can." Admit your fault if it is valid, and offer your apology and willingness to make amends.

If you are not at fault, don't become defensive. Try to explain as rationally as you can your role in the situation and that, though you were not responsible for the person's anger, you are willing to help in any way you can. Low-key nonverbal responses also help diffuse anger. People tend to see and hear things in an exaggerated way when they are angry, so a quiet tone of voice and relaxed but attentive posture can have a calming effect. Maintain steady eye contact while he vents his anger, and try not to interrupt. Letting him get it off his chest shows respect for his feelings and a willingness to cooperate to solve the problem. Listening to the other person, taking his feelings seriously, and remaining calm under pressure are all keys to successful communication.

Of course, if a person becomes violent or abusive, you should calmly tell him that you are willing to work out the problem, but you don't think it's a good time to continue the discussion right now. Then quietly leave. There's little more you can do in a situation like this.

Never be afraid to report abuse. One reason people continue verbal, emotional, and physical abuse is that no one stops them. It takes courage to stand up to an abuser, but it must be done, or the person will continue the same pattern.

In today's workplace, thousands of people fall victim to verbal and emotional abuse. Don't perpetuate it with silence. Recently, I found myself in a situation where I felt violated by the verbal exchange. I was so shocked by the language used that I had a delayed reaction. Three days after the event, I wrote a letter to the president of the organization and sent copies to the gentlemen who used the language. In the letter, I described the nature of our business meeting, how I felt about their choice of words, my need for the elimination of such language in future meetings, and the consequences of any repeated exchange. It never happened again.

How do you deal with anger that another person is holding in? If you feel that someone is angry with you, but he or she seems unwilling to be direct, there are three ways to respond.

First, you can closely examine what he is *not* saying, and try to determine the possible causes for his anger. If you can determine the cause and simply change something you are doing, you may be able to resolve the problem without confrontation. This is risky, however, because it may not be accurate and borders on mind reading.

Second, you can choose to ignore the negative messages being sent by a coworker, reasoning that if he really does have a problem with you, he can just come out and tell you. This is also risky because it does nothing to resolve the issue, which may only grow worse.

The final response is most appropriate. You may need a confrontation. You may not like it, but it is far more productive than letting a misunderstanding continue unchecked. Let the person know that it is safe to express anger by taking the initiative and telling him you feel something is wrong. Let him know that you are willing to work things out if you have done something to offend him. Most of the time, people appreciate a sincere effort to work out issues that can be resolved together. If that doesn't work and he is still angry, at least you've done your part. You can't force the other person to come forward.

There are practical ways to deal with anger. Let's go back to Victoria, the angry accountant mentioned earlier to see how she can apply these principles to the anger she experiences on her job.

Let go of petty annoyances. Victoria has some valid problems with the way the company is operating. However, things have reached the point where every small annoyance sets her teeth on edge. Although she certainly should express her concerns about what she sees as major flaws in the firm's operations, she is only feeding the flames of destructive anger by holding onto the smallest incident. By letting go of petty annoyances, she can focus constructively on the issues that should be addressed with her employer. Not only that, Victoria will also experience less stress if she is not on the lookout for one more minor incident to add to her stockpile of resentments.

Don't feed on others' anger. Victoria is not alone in her feelings of frustration and anger with her company. Several of her coworkers share those feelings, and her office is often the setting for discussions that center almost exclusively on what the company is doing wrong and how difficult it is to work there. Granted, it's only natural to want to let off some steam on occasion, but constant negative discussions accomplish nothing except to fuel the flames of discontent and hopelessness about the job situation.

Victoria would be better off directing her conversations with her coworkers to possible solutions. If those solutions have been ignored, as they have been in Victoria's case, then she and her coworkers should address that problem. Creating a sphere of positive influence with coworkers to bring about change is far more effective than running together in a vicious circle of faultfinding and complaining.

Watch what you say out of anger. Victoria has occasionally been careless about vocalizing her anger with the company and more than once has made comments that are inappropriate in her office setting. This could not only damage her growth in the company; it could hurt her credibility when she does present her concerns to management.

There is something to be said for the adage "bite the bullet," if it means you will keep from shooting yourself in the foot. Carefully choosing your words, even in the face of circumstances that cause justifiable anger, leaves your dignity and integrity intact, and keeps the doors of communication open.

Honest communication is key. One of Victoria's sources of anger comes from the fact that she has approached the company's management about her concerns and the response has been unsatisfactory. If you have been in the same situation, you know how frustrating it is when you feel ignored.

So what do you do? In Victoria's case, she can call a halt to the anger that's building inside and open an honest dialogue with her management, saying, "I'm concerned that perhaps we're not communicating clearly with each other. Can we sit down and further discuss the topics I've brought to your attention?" By confronting management in a way that is not defensive or negative, she would demonstrate persistence and subtly call for management to take some ownership in an exchange. Keeping the door of communication open will keep anger from building when other doors are closed.

Your attitude is the most important element in handling anger. It controls your response to anger and plays an important role in affecting other people's responses. Remember three things about anger: (1) it is OK to feel angry—it is your response that counts; (2) don't make important decisions while you're angry, as your ability to think rationally is impaired; and (3) don't make judgments about people while either you or they are angry. Instead, concentrating on how you can change yourself and your own responses will make anger a lot easier to handle.

The Give-and-Take of Criticism

There is an alarming situation arising in American business because of the negative approach to giving and taking criticism. For example, one of the top causes of job stress is a lack of feedback, especially criticism. The two major reasons executives lose their jobs are because of insensitivity to others and an inability to allow for the views of others.[1]

Many people respond negatively to the word criticism, instantly associating it with harsh comments, hurt feelings, and angry responses.

But criticism does not have to be destructive, regardless whether you are on the giving or the receiving end. Instead, criticism can serve as a useful tool for improving job performance, motivating others, and creating a sense of ownership as solutions are reached.

In order to understand positive criticism, however, we need to look at negative criticism. Be conscious of the spirit in which criticism is given. Are you prone to negative criticism? Ask yourself if you have lost perspective and humor because you are so focused on what others are doing wrong. Remember that if you are too critical, you are blocking the creative process that accompanies any job. Being critical in a negative way inhibits good relationships, produces retaliatory criticism, and bruises much-needed good will among coworkers.

A negative critic will find himself talking about a coworker behind his back, which fosters distrust and anger once that coworker finds out it is happening.

- Negative criticism attacks. It says, "Do you really think you're going to get anywhere doing work like this?"
- Negative criticism threatens. "You'd better get on the stick with your computer skills or there will be some repercussions."
- Negative criticism insults. "How much time did you spend on your presentation? It was awful."
- Negative criticism embarrasses. "Hey, guys, let's put Debbie's work on the bulletin board as an example of what *not* to do."

You get the picture. In fact, that is the sort of criticism demonstrated by Terry, the systems analyst at the beginning of the chapter. Negative criticism is a destructive force that can cause irreparable damage to self-esteem, job productivity, and attitude. On the "Why You Hate Your Job" list, it ranks on top for a lot of employees. But criticism doesn't have to get a bad rap. Indeed, there are ways to criticize productively.

Think of it as teaching. You have information that can help someone learn how to produce better work. When you share that information, you are serving as an instructor of sorts. For example, you might say, "You did a good job! Am I right in thinking you didn't have as much time to present that excellent information as you would have liked? Let's get together and talk about how you can format the information so that next time you can discuss each point in more detail within the time period." You've just taught your coworker, through criticism, how to improve on his or her job.

Build self-esteem. Letting a coworker know that his work is valuable is a true self-esteem builder. When you tell him he is doing a good job, he will most likely be far more receptive to hearing how he can do an even better job next time.

Criticism means caring. People *can* feel that you care when you criticize. By expressing your concern, you are saying, "I care if you succeed on your job. Let me share with you a way that can boost your success."

Timing can be everything. You do not want to pick a moment when a coworker is already depressed about something to get involved in a discussion that can fuel negativity or defensiveness.

Consider the setting, your own emotions, and whether others are present. Also, be sure the recipient can do something about the situation you are offering criticism about. If it is too late to do anything about the situation, he or she will only become frustrated.

Be specific. Vague criticisms can create a chasm of anxiety and doubt. Don't leave the recipient guessing; give an example of where she may be falling short and what you think she can do to improve.

Listen. How does the recipient of your criticism feel afterward? Ask. Then listen closely to determine if she understands what you have said and how she is feeling about it.

Avoid the "shoulds." How are you coming across? Are the first words out of your mouth, "You know, you really should write your reports this way"? When you remain open and instructive, instead of rigid and pedantic, your criticism is far more likely to gain acceptance.

Don't push. Pushing the person you're criticizing to take your suggested action puts stress on the recipient and shows that you are far more concerned with seeing your suggestions implemented than your coworkers' well-being.

When possible, consider temperaments. The command-person will not respond to criticism in the same way the support-person will. Keep in mind that a sensitive coworker could require a more delicate approach, whereas the matter-of-fact colleague will value a tactful, yet more direct, discussion.

Talk about rewards. Tell the person that you are criticizing *how* he will benefit from taking a certain action. There is nothing like reminding someone of the powerful payoffs that can come as a result of responding positively to a criticism.

Now that you know how to give criticism, how do you take it? Take a brief look at something you do that could cause someone to criticize you. Maybe you make mistakes. Mess-ups, miscalculations, failures, just plain, "I blew its!" are bound to happen. But, like anger, it's the way you respond to the mistakes that makes the difference.

First of all, it is important to remember to take responsibility for your failures as well as your successes. Look at the mistakes and failures as necessary and valuable life lessons, and don't let your response to them (and the resultant criticism) sabotage the rest of your work life.

Realize that successful people actually make more mistakes than unsuccessful people. What that means is that successful people keep trying far longer than unsuccessful people who quit or give up after a few failures. Successful people know that a spectacular success will justify all the failures along the way. How many tries do you think it took Thomas Edison to get the light bulb or the phonograph right? Don't be afraid to fail or make a mistake, and don't be afraid to own up to it.

Don't let mistakes weigh you down. You may go through periods where you make more mistakes than at other times. The greater the stress of the situation, the greater the chance of making mistakes. But remember to be patient with yourself, forgive yourself, and look to your successes to define you, not your failures.

You have admitted that you made a mistake, you have forgiven yourself, and you are ready to move on. But here comes the boss or coworker anxious to share a few "suggestions" about what you did and how it could be handled better in the future.

How do you take the criticism?

Be willing to learn. You can take an active stance and ask others how you can improve and then be open to what they say. If you realize that criticism is a way to help you measure and improve performance on the job, you'll welcome it.

Listen and learn. Even if you have not sought the correction or criticism, turn off the tendency to respond defensively, and truly listen to the criticism. If it is productive criticism, try to respond positively in return.

Do not put yourself down. Be kind to yourself. Don't decide that you have totally botched the project because someone has pointed out a way it could be improved for future presentations. Don't decide that you are a total failure at work because one suggestion has been made on how you can work more effectively in the future.

Ask for more. Once you are comfortable with receiving criticism, express gratitude for the help, then ask for more suggestions.

Anger and *criticism*—those two words with negative connotations—can be handled in a way that produces good results on your job. You may have to return to this chapter for a healthy reminder that out of confrontations can come tremendous growth.

Coping with a Job Loss

14

Whitney, a project coordinator for an event planning firm, never saw it coming. She was called into her supervisor's office, and fifteen minutes later she was walking down the hall to her cubicle—jobless. Stunned and dazed, she managed to pack her personal items and leave the building, wondering through the haze of confusion what she would do now.

Months later, Whitney was still unemployed, with the added burden of mounting debt and, worse still, increasing depression over losing a job she had come to love.

The loss of a job creates a wide range of strong emotions: fear, anger, depression, panic, guilt, anxiety, grief, and more. Even in a situation where someone is less than enthusiastic about his job, the effect on his self-image can be distressing. But when you have come to love the job you once hated, coping strategies are essential to a successful comeback from the crisis.

Before we examine the course to take if you find yourself in a situation similar to Whitney's, let's look at the circumstances surrounding a dismissal from a job.

The unexpected nature of a dismissal may prevent the employee from probing into the reasons why he or she was let go. It would help the employee to know if it was actually the company's fault. In fact, *99 percent of firing is really the company's fault.*[1]

The mistakes a company makes that lead to an employee's termination are varied and include bad planning, bad administering, bad strategies, bad hiring as well as poor training, poor supervision, and poor follow-up.[2] Unfortunately, the employee experiences a great deal of unnecessary pain because he or she is unaware of those problems.

Also according to *Boardroom Reports*, "Companies often fire people because of 'laziness.' In fact, very few people perceived as lazy really are. It's actually very hard work to spend an entire day doing nothing. Managers must look closer at the reason for an employee's underperformance. It usually has something to do with the way he/she is being managed." [3]

If you have been laid off not because you didn't do your job adequately, but because your *company* made mistakes, the company should treat you with special concern. While the pain of dismissal is still substantial, you should be able to leave knowing you gave your best to the job and that the company bears the responsibility for your leaving. In other words, it's their loss!

Even if your termination is the result of your poor performance, the following things should precede your dismissal if your company has attempted to be fair to you:

- **Confrontation**—regular confrontation by the supervisor regarding your performance problems
- **Memos**—regular memos from the supervisor about your mistakes
- **Training**—regular training in order to improve your performance
- **Switches**—a move from the present position to one that is better-suited to your abilities. [4]

Losing the Job You Love

In Whitney's case her company was at fault. It wasn't able to sustain the number of its employees because it had grown quickly—too quickly—and, because of bad management, was teetering on the brink of financial disaster. The easy solution was to let some of its employees go.

If you are like Whitney, a self-described "workaholic," the loss of a job is like having a part of yourself cut off. Although the term workaholic seems to have negative connotations, that's more likely an undeserved bad rap. Many of this ilk are dedicated and enthusiastic; they are people who should be immensely valuable to their companies. As one description summarizes, "workaholics" are:

those whose desire to work long and hard is intrinsic and whose
work habits almost always exceed the prescriptions of the job they
do and the expectations of the people with whom or for whom they
work. But the first characteristic is the real determinant. What truly
distinguishes the workaholics from other hard workers is that others
work only to please a boss, earn a promotion, or meet a deadline. . . .
For workaholics on the other hand, the workload seldom lightens,
for they don't want to work less. [my emphasis][5]

Whitney experienced the sense of being lost to the point that she became practically immobilized after several weeks of fruitless job searching. Her self-esteem suffered, her desire to continue looking for a job dwindled with each rejection letter, and her mounting frustration was turning to bitterness.

What can you do when you lose the job you love? How can you cope? Following are some methods to help you deal with the painful separation from a job that has become the driving force in your life.

Grieve

Mourn the job that was so important to you. As with any loss, it is only natural to want to give in to the pain of separation. Many studies over the years have shown that job loss is high on the list of traumatic life experiences. Allow yourself to experience the tears, the anger, and the *grief* over losing your job. Otherwise, you will find yourself denying the pain of the event. Denial creates a web of self-deception that can eventually trap you into destructive depression and rage.

Although there is no set time frame for the grieving period, it is important to note that if you find yourself experiencing a lasting feeling of helplessness and hopelessness, and if your grief has deepened into paralyzing depression, you should seek counseling from a pastor or professional counselor. The purpose of grieving is to purge and eventually put the strong initial emotions behind you. If the grief only grows, you may want to find someone who is concerned and objective to help you deal with it.

Put the Job in Perspective

If you are like Whitney, you don't know where the job begins and you end. You and your job have become one. Your identity has become so deeply entwined with the job that you feel anonymous without it. There is a lack of balance and perspective in your life.

While joblessness is very uncomfortable, and certainly not an ideal situation, it may be a positive turning point. Now you can ask yourself, *Have I been consumed with this job to the exclusion of family, personal life, friends, spiritual, physical, or emotional growth?* Often, a deep attachment to a job reflects a struggle with self-esteem—the job compensates for what you perceive as a lack of ability or strength in other areas of your life. As you review the chapters on self-esteem, you may want to pursue more personal growth by talking to your pastor or counselor and spending time in prayer and meditation.

It is important to feel fulfilled in your job. But when the job replaces other components necessary to a healthy lifestyle, it is time to get a new perspective.

Confront Your Role in the Job Loss

Now is not the time to beat yourself up, but if any self-evaluation is called for, do it as soon as you are comfortable with the idea. Most likely, your company let you go because, like Whitney's company, they made some mistakes that you are paying for. But if your job performance played a part in your dismissal, look at it squarely and determine how you can best improve the next time around.

This is a vulnerable time for you, so be gentle with yourself. Don't constantly berate yourself about the things that can stand improvement. Just because you are examining your job performance doesn't mean you place yourself under a microscope of criticism. Continue to remind yourself of the things you did well—your dedication, accomplishments, successes, and so on.

Find a Reason to Get Up Every Day

You may be feeling like Whitney—discouraged over the length of time it's taking to get a new job. But you won't want to give in to the inertia that can begin to plague your job search.

In order to beat the increasing desire to pull the covers over your head and stay in bed, decide to set and meet at least one goal for yourself everyday. Preferably, the goals involve your job search: making phone calls, sending out resumes, reading the want ads, networking, and so on. But if it takes deciding that you just want to see a movie, or take your shaggy pet to the groomer, by all means, let that goal get you started.

The idea is to keep moving—not to the point of exhaustion but to maintain the habit of daily activity that you developed when you were working. Your activities may have changed, but you can still be productive, and the end result can eventually be a new job that you love.

Join a Support Group

If you don't have a group of unemployed persons in your community who meet to talk about their experiences, form one! Unfortunately, not many places in the country have *not* been forced to tighten their personnel belts. So there are probably many people who would respond to your ad in the paper about forming such a group.

Support groups are not meant to create a "misery loves company" situation. The best groups provide encouragement, education, and feedback to one another as they face a shared difficult situation together. You can create friendships, take your mind off yourself by concentrating on the needs of others, and even discover new opportunities in employment that you may not have considered.

Keep the Lines of Communication Open

Spouses, children, friends, family members—those who are most concerned about your well-being are often the very ones you avoid talking to. Don't bury your feelings of stress or depression. If you don't share your concerns, you will feel even more stressed.

Give mini-progress reports on your job search—before you're asked. That way, you won't feel that you are being pinned down each and every day to tell everyone how things are going. If you know someone who can relay your progress through the grapevine, all the better.

More Coping Strategies

Don't Expect Too Much from Yourself

Although it is definitely important to set daily goals for yourself, try not to overdo it. If you are a classic workaholic, you will put as much drive into your job search as you did into your job. But don't go into overload. Balance your day with activities that don't require a lot of mental energy, which will help to minimize stress.

Exercise

It may require more energy than you think you have to exercise, but it can make a difference in your stress level at this time. Even a moderate exercise program releases endorphins, which lift your spirits and give you a sense of control over depression.[6]

Beware of Overeating or Drinking

If you find yourself heading far too often toward the ice cream container or the local bar, consider what's driving your behavior. Fear? Anxiety? Depression? All of the above? It's only natural to seek comfort and relaxation during the stressful time of joblessness, but self-awareness in the areas of excessive eating and drinking is crucial to avoiding problems down the road. If you are unable to stop yourself, do not be afraid to seek help.

Seek Comfort in Meditation and Prayer

Meditation and prayer can be a source of peace during your time of joblessness (and other times). Reading the Bible and other inspirational materials can provide a sense of calm and hope.

Recognize That There Will Be an End to This

No one can guarantee when you will get the job you want (or even one you don't want). But you will be able to approach each day with a proactive attitude if you remind yourself that this challenging time will come to an end and that your diligence and persistence can pay off in a new job situation.

New Job Strategies

Once you're no longer in your old job, usually your top priority is to get a new job. The following are some strategies you can use to help you handle this unexpected change in your career.

The Resume

You've probably been in the job market long enough to learn how to put together a resume, so we won't spend a lot of time on this. But you can do a few things to get your resume read.

- If you can afford it, have someone typeset and design it. Many small design firms and print shops will take your information and create a resume that is attractive without being too slick and will grab the attention of your intended audience. Color, type, layout—all these elements can come together to create a memorable resume.
- Create several resumes. If you want to stress several skills, don't depend on one resume to do the job. Take the time to emphasize one aspect of your former position over others. For instance, Whitney did much of the writing and designing in her position at the event planning firm, but she was also involved in sales. She created two different resumes highlighting the duties and accomplishments of one of those skills over the other in each one, depending on the position she was applying for.
- Treat your resume as your ambassador. Your resume will speak for you, so make it reader friendly and full of your positive accomplishments. Like an ambassador, it deserves dignity, not desperation; don't send it all over town to places and people you really don't have an interest in. That's a waste of time and energy—yours and people you're sending it to.

Contacts, Contacts, Contacts

Think of former bosses, coworkers, and clients. Friends of friends—even your dentist. Contacts are more important than ever, now that many companies are eliminating the use of employment agencies and executive search firms. Many companies today rely instead on employee referrals, so stay in touch with as many people as you can throughout your job search. Companies are staying away from mass media, help wanted ads in order to target qualified people, so contacts can be a crucial way to hear of job openings.[7]

Seek Career Counseling

If you feel like you're floundering in your search, consider career counseling. You will not only have a sounding board for your frustrations, more important, you will have sound, objective recommendations and qualified guidance, particularly if you plan to head in a new career direction.

Changing Careers?

If you are looking at your job loss as an opportunity to pursue another career course, good for you. Here are a few items to check off as you make plans for the change.

- Put yourself to the test. There are a lot of self-test books on the market now that can help you determine a new direction. A career counselor is also able to provide tests that can help you determine what or if that new career is for you.
- Explore your options. Doing a little informal research can be beneficial. Talk to people who are involved in the area that you are thinking of moving into. Learning from them will give you a head start into your new job field.
- Start training. If you can afford to take some courses in your new career, do so. Even if you're basically qualified, training can help polish your skills even more and help you feel as if you are already involved in your new career.
- Cover your bases with a cover letter. This is probably more important than your resume because this letter will discuss why you want to make the move into a new career. It also gives you an opportunity to explain more in depth how your skills and accomplishments can translate into your new position.

Stay on Course

After several months of unemployment, Whitney was fast approaching the point of taking *any* job. That is not always the best approach. You may find that subsequent employers will wonder why you couldn't do better, and brief blocks of time on jobs that are unrelated to your career make you look disloyal and flighty. Instead, consider the following alternatives.

- Join a temporary agency. You can continue looking for a position while you're working part- or full-time with an agency. Once an opportunity comes along, you will be free to take it and leave without a blemish on your resume (or your conscience).
- Consider freelancing. If your job skills allow it, fill in for someone who has left his job temporarily on parental leave or sabbatical, for instance. Freelancing on projects provides an income, and isn't quite as restrictive as temporary work for an agency. However, it carries more responsibility in the form of taxes and marketing yourself to potential employers.
- Transfer your skills. Decide what transferable skills you have, then look for a job at your level in one of the industries that has not suffered major damage from present economic conditions, such as environmental protection or waste management. You will be able to broaden your skills, and when a job in your chosen field comes along, you will be even more valuable to a prospective employer. [8]

If You Are Facing a Layoff

Trisha, a sales rep for a national blue chip firm, had a little more warning than Whitney. The rumors of layoffs at her company had rumbled through the media and the corporation for months. But when she was let go, she still did not feel prepared somehow. She had only recently thought about updating her resume, making a few contacts, and considering career options. Although Trisha would be the first to admit that she didn't especially like her job, losing it still came as a blow to her self-esteem.

First of all, be sure you are actually being laid off. Very often, the company is firing you but calling it a layoff. A layoff implies that at some point you could be rehired. Being fired means you are permanently dismissed from the company. Among other things that are affected by this difference in terminology could be your unemployment benefits.

Like Trisha, the millions of people who have been laid off during tough economic times or because a company has merged, may have disliked—even hated—their jobs. Nevertheless, they experience the same sense of devastation, fear, and depression that those who have been terminated feel. Most of the information in this chapter is as relevant to the person who has been laid off as to the one who has been fired. There are, however, a few things for the person who has been laid off to keep in mind.

Be Prepared

Trisha had the best intentions, but she didn't quite follow through on her plans once the rumors got started about the coming layoffs in her company. Updating a resume, considering new career options, networking—these were steps Trisha could have taken to help her advance more quickly through the jobless stage and feel more confident about being ready for the changes.

Find Out the Facts

You've heard the rumors. But perhaps you can find out for sure. Nothing is more stressful than hearing bits and pieces of what might happen, drifting through corporate halls. You want the straight facts, so go to whatever reliable source you have—a supervisor, personnel director—whoever can help you sort out truth from fiction.

Think—Then Talk about Your Options

Your company is considering letting you go. But would they consider moving you into another position within the company? Do you have the kind of position where you can subcontract with them? Don't just decide that you're leaving. If management is willing to listen, talk to them about how you can benefit them in other ways if you stay with the firm.

Can You Become Indispensable?

They say no one is indispensable. But when it comes to the bottom line, if you are able to position yourself as being able to help the company regain profitability, then you are rapidly approaching being indispensable. Remember, though, that it is vital that you be able to follow through on your promises.

Start Your Own Business

Whether you have a little or a lot of lead time before you're laid off, you can take steps toward starting your own company. We've already mentioned subcontracting with your old company, but you can also develop a broad base of customers to help build a successful business.

Think Worst-case Scenario

That may sound negative, but actually, your fears and anxieties will probably head you in that direction anyway—so why not meet them head-on? By thinking about the worst case that can happen once you're laid off, you gain a measure of control. After all, you will have envisioned the major problem; now you can prepare the solutions. Considering all the alternatives can improve your position, whatever the actual circumstances (and usually, the worst-case scenario never materializes anyway).

Hopefully, you will never have to cope with a job loss. But if you do, take heart: you can make it through this difficult time armed with the strategies discussed, as well as the faith that comes from knowing that this, too, shall pass.

Special Section for Employers (Employees can read it too!)

The High Cost of Low Self-Esteem

15

How much of an impact does low self-esteem have on an employer's bottom line? The average American worker puts in about 140 more hours per year on the job than he or she did two decades ago.[1] Businesses are finding that cutting too many workers can lead to losing customers and experience and destroy employee morale.[2] Add low self-esteem and its negative effects to the situation and you have a potential disaster for American businesses.

A recent *Newsweek* survey asked Americans how important self-esteem is in motivating a person to work hard and succeed.[3] Eighty-nine percent responded that self-esteem is very important. Status in the eyes of others was very important to only 35 percent of the respondents. That implies that others' opinions of our success are not as important as our own opinion of our success. Perhaps that is why many people do not find satisfaction in the trappings of status. They still feel the effects of low self-esteem.

What does that suggest for employers who need to motivate fewer employees to be even more productive? It suggests that the most effective motivation may be efforts that foster healthy self-esteem. We will examine that more closely in chapter 18; in this chapter, you will see how low self-esteem in the workplace is costing you money—lots of it.

How Low Self-Esteem in the Workplace Costs Employers Money

Healthcare Costs

The area of greatest loss is in healthcare costs. In 1970, total health services and supplies expenditures were $69.1 billion. Of that amount, including contribution of private health insurance premiums, businesses spent $15.1 billion. In 1990, total expenditures increased to $643.4 billion, with businesses paying $186.2 billion. That represents an increase of more than 900 percent for the nation and more than 1200 percent for businesses.[4] By the year 2000, healthcare may cost the nation more than $1.7 trillion, consuming 18 percent of the nation's economic output.[5]

Absenteeism

The National Center for Health Statistics shows that for every hundred employees, employers lose about 10 months of workdays a year to sicknesses and injuries. However, studies show that the costs of absenteeism go far beyond payments for sick leave. Direct costs, such as paying for sick leave, average $411 per employee per year, but that amount does not include the following: overtime paid to cover unscheduled absences, temporary help to fill in for absent employees, time spent rearranging work schedules, time spent by absentees catching up when they return, decreased morale and productivity of workers who have to compensate for absentees, and lost revenue from customer dissatisfaction caused by poor service.[6]

Drug and Alcohol Addiction and Mental Health Problems

People with low self-esteem do not cope with stress effectively. They have a much greater tendency to resort to drugs, alcohol, and other addictive behavior to attempt to cope with stress. They also have a greater tendency to experience mental and emotional health problems, such as depression, that require some form of professional treatment.

The cost of treating addictions is actually far less than the cost of treating medical problems that result from leaving them untreated. The daily cost of treating addiction is only one-half to one-fifth the daily cost of treating illnesses such as cirrhosis, high blood pressure, strokes, and trauma resulting from untreated addictions.[7] Studies also show medical (non-psychiatric) inpatient hospitalization can be reduced by 60 to 88 percent when patients receive psychotherapy.[8]

The average addict or mental health sufferer who continues to work without getting treatment costs the company about $7,500 a year for the following reasons: he uses 3 times the medical benefits, has 2.5 times the number of 8-day or longer absences, makes 5 times the workman's compensation claims, has 3.6 times the number of accidents, is late to work 3 times as often, and requests time off 2.2 times as often as the healthy coworker.[9]

About 20 percent of employees also suffer from codependency, the disabling emotional or mental stress resulting from living with an addict. Firing addicted or codependent employees is an expensive way to deal with this problem since the cost of recruiting and training new staff is increasing every year. Doing so could also violate the Americans with Disabilities Act of 1992.[10] (Handling employees with drug or alcohol and mental health problems will be discussed in more detail in chapter 16.)

Education, Training, and Retraining

An estimated 15 million adults holding jobs are functionally illiterate. That means $225 billion in lost productivity.[11] Research shows that 80 percent of businesses say their employees' writing skills need improvement, and 75 percent say their interpersonal skills need improvement. Yet only 21 percent of these companies say they offer programs to improve writing, and only 25 percent have formal literacy programs. The most prevalent programs are management and leadership training at 70 percent, computer training at 67 percent and interpersonal communications training at 42 percent.[12]

Though it is commendable that businesses are willing to offer so much management and computer training, there is a serious need to offer, subsidize, and encourage other more basic skills. With the large influx of minorities and immigrants into the work force, businesses must be prepared to help meet the educational needs of those who must overcome economic, cultural, or language barriers. Even those at the lower levels of the organization must be included because, "In the new economy, individuals at all levels of the company and in all kinds of companies are challenged to develop new knowledge and to create new value, to take responsibility for their ideas and to pursue them as far as they can go."[13]

Keeping these people is especially critical in light of the cost of hiring and training employees. In small businesses, which make up 70 percent of businesses in the United States, the cost can be devastating. In a 2 to 3 million dollar business that is netting 1 or 2 percent after taxes, when an employee starts at $30,000 plus benefits and leaves six months later, about half the company's profit is lost on one trainee.[14]

Ergonomics

Were the desks and chairs in your office originally designed for white males? If they are based on older proportions, they are likely too big and uncomfortable for females and persons of different ethnic characteristics, such as smaller Asians. Are your computers placed on tables or desks that were not made for computers? If so, they may cause repetitive stress injuries such as carpal tunnel syndrome.

Ergonomics, or the study of how individuals interact with their work environment, was discussed in chapter 11, but the results of poorly designed work environments can cost employers thousands of dollars in healthcare and worker's compensation. These kinds of injuries reached 56 percent of work-related claims in 1990 and, considering that more than one-third of U.S. workers operate office computers, these claims are likely to increase. They already cost employers $20 billion in 1990.[15]

How do these problems relate to self-esteem? Employees with low self-esteem, who believe that management will not do anything to rectify these situations, will probably continue to tolerate them. They will end up costing the company money. Employees with a level of self-esteem that makes them conscientious about their health will be more likely to leave a company that they feel does not care about their needs. It is essential for a business to keep abreast of potential problems in the work environment and make sure employees know the company wants to correct them.

Productivity

People with a high level of self-esteem often say they feel productive. People with low self-esteem say they do not feel productive and lack incentives to be productive.

The common remedies for dealing with the changing economic environment and global competition, such as downsizing, re-engineering, and outsourcing, have all failed to realize the most valuable of the nation's competitive resources: knowledge. As one writer for the *Harvard Business Review* expressed it, "The revolution in information and communications technologies makes knowledge the new competitive resource. But knowledge only flows through the technology; it actually resides in people. . . . In the end, the location of the new economy is not in the technology, be it the microchip or the global communications network. It is in the human mind."[16]

As an example of the "old economy" and its way of ignoring workers' needs and ideas, consider General Motors. John DeLorean shocked the business world when he resigned as a vice president in 1973 and revealed many of the inside problems at the automotive giant in subsequent books.

To compete with Ford's Pinto in the mini-car market, GM introduced the Vega in 1970. The design recommended by the Chevrolet engineers was ignored in favor of a design put together by corporate management. DeLorean, who was head of Chevrolet at the time, described the engine design:

What resulted was a relatively large, noisy, top-heavy combination of aluminum and iron which cost far too much to build, looked like it had been taken off a 1920 farm tractor and weighed more than the cast iron engine Chevy had proposed, or the foreign built, four-cylinder iron engine the Ford Pinto was to use. Chevy engineers were ashamed of the engine . . . [and] were almost totally disinterested in the car.[17]

But DeLorean had to motivate his workers to produce the car. He told them, "Like it or not, we are going to be building and selling this car. Any way you look at it, this car is going into the market as a Chevrolet. We can't put a little notice in the glove box saying 'We didn't design this car, Central Staff did.' It's a Chevrolet, and we are going to be responsible to the public for how good a car we build and sell."[18] By inspiring his workers to take pride in what they built, DeLorean was able to make the Vega one of the best quality cars ever produced by GM, despite its engine design problems, which ultimately resulted in the car's downfall.

Before leaving GM, DeLorean wrote a memo with his recommendations for improving profit at the company. Number one on his list was "Better management, management motivation & morale," which he estimated would improve potential profit by $200 million.[19] Workers who are motivated to have high self-esteem and allowed to take pride in their work offer the greatest source of productivity and profit potential a business can have.

GM is learning, if slowly, from its mistakes. A positive example is the GM Harrison Division where workers ranging from mid-level executives to secretaries to engineers are being encouraged to find better ways to do their jobs. In 1990, the plant's manufacturing engineering staff launched about 20 cost-reduction and time-saving projects, cutting 33,000 hours a year of engineering time. A simplified order form reduced the tool ordering process from 11 days to 1 day. Though GM is cutting 20,000 jobs from its overall white collar workforce by 1995, the time-saving procedures at the Harrison plant have not resulted in any layoffs and have actually allowed the staff to take on many new projects.[20]

Two keys to the effectiveness of the GM Harrison Division procedures have been identified: 1) managers' willingness to surrender power to employees, and 2) employees' willingness to trust managers.[21] That leads to the crucial point of understanding the high cost of low self-esteem. Managers and employees alike cannot function in this new system effectively with low self-esteem, yet, as we are seeing more and more in the business world, this model is a necessity to survival. Low self-esteem and resulting insecurity causes the manager to fear losing authority; therefore, it is difficult if not impossible to empower employees. Low self-esteem also cripples employees' ability to trust those in authority; as they are used to being taken advantage of and even abused. Both must work toward a team concept that strengthens self-esteem, pride in the work, job satisfaction, and ultimate profitability.

The Team Concept

W. Edwards Deming, the father of quality management who helped postwar Japan make its economic turnaround, taught that businesses must adopt a new philosophy. This philosophy has been called by various terms, including empowerment, teamwork, partnership, and coaching, but the bottom line is trust. As Alan Webber stated after reviewing numerous current business books for the *Harvard Business Review*, "All of these authors agree that in the new economy, trust is a business imperative. Trust between managers and workers opens up new avenues of contribution and responsibility on both sides."[22]

Trust is difficult to achieve. Managers fear vulnerability, loss of control and authority, conflict, and disagreement. That is why many companies have preferred to manage by numbers, or quotas, rather than building trust and teamwork. But Webber says, "If that strategy seemed to work in the past, managers can no longer afford its *high costs* [italics mine]. Indeed, healthy conflict is a sign of the existence of trust. It shows two people care enough about what they are doing together to disagree."[23]

Therefore, it is now management's role to "attract and motivate the best people; reward, recognize, and retain them; train, educate, and improve them; ... [even] serve and satisfy them."[24] It is management's job to build trusting relationships and empower employees to perform effectively in those relationships. This will lead to healthier self-esteem for both managers and workers and, ultimately, a healthier business.

The question is, just how does management begin to build a relationship of trust? Here are some suggestions to get your company started.

Develop a Mission Statement

Thoroughly examine your markets and your products and services for those markets. Determine a long-term vision for your company (or department) that seeks to position you as the most profitable solution to those market needs. Consider all your company resources for fulfilling those needs, especially your human resources. Then mold the vision into a clearly defined purpose that employees can understand and embrace.

Encourage Employees to Refine the Mission Statement

The best way to do this is to involve employees in the development of the mission statement. Consult them for their visions and knowledge of the company's markets and resources, particularly frontline workers who deal with your customers every day. Then publish the statement, make sure everyone has a copy, and show continual support for it so that your employees will work with you as a team to fulfill the mission.

Conduct Regular Employee Surveys

A recent survey of more than fourteen hundred companies revealed that 28 percent of them had never conducted a formal employee attitude survey. Forty-four percent indicated that top management wished neither to ask about nor respond to employee concerns.[25] There are many outside consultants who will conduct an impartial survey of your company's workers and present the information in a detailed analysis. Most management consultants recommend doing these surveys periodically. "The best-run and most respected companies in America . . . [such as] Disney and Merck, conduct regular employee surveys and use the information to guide them in organizing and managing their people. The benefits range widely, and include . . . flaws in operational procedures, and suggestions for improving efficiency and productivity."[26]

Institute Team Training

Management needs to learn how to create teams. They must also learn how to empower the teams, allow employees to make decisions, and support their efforts. They must teach employees how to take ownership for the company and its operations. It is more important for management to listen to employees' ideas and facilitate team meetings and plans than to give direction.

Institute a Vigorous Program of Education and Self-Improvement

This is Deming's point number 13 in his 14-point quality message. The more you can invest in employees' development, the less you will have to invest in other, more expensive costs such as lost sales and lower productivity, turnover and rehiring, and stress-related illnesses and injuries.

Drive Out Fear So That Everyone May Work Effectively for the Company

This is Deming's point number 8. Management must create an emotional atmosphere where people are secure enough to ask tough questions and to ask for help when they need it. They must not be afraid of losing their jobs if they do so. That is essential to developing trust. "In an environment where we must have every good idea from every man and woman in the organization, we cannot afford management styles that suppress and intimidate."[27] The key is for managers to learn how to ask for honest feedback and facilitate communication. The more managers strive to understand their employees' work and personal needs and value their participation in running the company, the more fear is reduced, trust is built, and satisfaction and commitment are increased.

Offer All the Support Programs You Can for Your Employees

Whatever kinds of support programs you can provide to help employees cope with the stress of the daily work environment will greatly benefit the company. It is far cheaper to institute wellness programs, stress-management programs, Employee Assistance Programs, employee satisfaction surveys, and self-improvement programs than to pay the staggering costs that result when no such programs are available.

The high cost of low self-esteem translates into billions of dollars that are lost by American businesses every year. This chapter gives specific examples of some of these costs and how they are related to low self-esteem. There is an even higher cost, in terms of national pride. Many American products have gained a reputation for low quality, and American businesses have gained a reputation for greed and indifference to the environment as well as to the needs of workers, customers, and their communities. Now is the time, even if only for practical survival reasons, that American business must begin to address these needs and contribute to a better social as well as economic environment. Fortunately, there are many companies, both large and small, that have already begun.

How to Love the Employee You Hate

16

There are tests to evaluate potential employees and analyze everything from intelligence to sales ability. You can go over a resume or job application with a fine-tooth comb. You can check references from previous employers and personal acquaintances. Yet, you can still end up with an employee who drives you crazy for a multitude of reasons. The following anonymous fictional evaluation of several job applicants illustrates this point.

To: Jesus, Son of Joseph
        Woodcrafter Carpenter Shop
        Nazareth 25922
From: Jordan Management Consultants
        Jerusalem 26544
Re: Results of Personality Evaluations

Thank you for submitting resumes of the twelve men you have selected for management positions in your new organization. All have taken our battery of tests. We have run their results through our computer and have made evaluations from the personal interviews each person had with our psychologist and our vocational aptitude consultant. We are enclosing the profiles of each test and urge you to review them carefully.

In addition to our regular reports, we are also presenting a few general comments derived from our staff consultants and evaluations on some of the nominees. There is no additional cost for this service.

It is our considered opinion that most of your nominees are seriously lacking in background, education and vocational aptitude for your enterprise as we understand it. They do not show any evidence of having a "team concept," an essential trait. Frankly, we recommend that you continue your search for capable persons who

have had relevant experience and who can demonstrate proven
management skills and capabilities.

Simon Peter is emotionally unstable, showing fits of temper and
accompanying irrationality.

Andrew is entirely devoid of leadership ability.

The brothers James and John, the sons of Zebedee, apparently
place their personal interests above company loyalty.

Thomas exhibits an attitude of questioning and disbelief,
something certain to undermine morale.

We also feel you should be aware that Matthew has been officially
blacklisted by the Greater Jerusalem Better Business Bureau,
apparently for good cause.

James, son of Alpheus, and Thaddeus showed definite radical
urges and tendencies, as well as achieving inordinately high scores
on the manic-depressive scale.

However, one of your candidates shows great potential. He is a
man of ability and great resourcefulness, seems to be truly
people-oriented, shows a business acumen, and has contacts in high
places. He tested as being highly motivated, ambitious and
responsible. We would recommend that Judas Iscariot become your
controller, if not your most trusted associate.

All other profiles are self-explanatory. We wish you every success
in your new venture.

Sincerely yours,
The Jordan Management Group

Of course, we all know how trustworthy Judas turned out to be!
Even a battery of tests couldn't predict that outcome. Actually, aptitude
and personality testing are on the rise in businesses today. According
to the Administrative Management Society, 40 percent of service
businesses, 50 percent of banking and finance businesses and 73
percent of utilities and transportation businesses are now using these
evaluation techniques.[1] So why do you still end up with employees
who test well but end up being a problem?

A Story of Promising Talent

Sheila was promoted to manager of a staff of three attorneys in a
small legal counseling firm. From the beginning, Sheila was aware that
Kevin was her brightest and most talented attorney, despite his young

age. She assigned him cases that required innovative thinking, and she was usually rewarded with satisfied clients.

While another attorney was on vacation, Sheila had to assign Kevin a case with a client who was a bit more conservative than he was used to handling. When he presented the results of his research and his recommendation to Sheila, she knew the client would not accept it. She explained to Kevin that his work was excellent but he needed to make some revisions to accommodate the client. To her shock, the normally gentle and soft-spoken Kevin exploded. He vented an emotional tirade nothing short of a temper tantrum and stomped sulkily off to his office.

Stunned by his behavior, Sheila asked one of the other attorneys whether she had ever seen Kevin display such behavior before. The woman told her that Kevin was usually easy to get along with, but on occasion he did lash out with bursts of temper that seemed unexplainable. Later, he acted as if nothing had ever happened and was even surprised that anyone was upset with him. He had even been reprimanded a few times by his former supervisor, but the behavior still occurred. He seemed to have a reputation as a somewhat absent-minded genius whose sometimes peculiar behavior was tolerated because of his excellent work.

Sheila talked with Kevin. His self-esteem was suffering badly because of these problems. Sheila began to suspect that Kevin may have a deeper problem that even he was not aware of. She assured him that he was a valuable employee, whose talent and dedication she did not want to lose. She suggested he get professional counseling.

After several sessions with a psychologist and some diagnostic tests, the mystery was solved. Kevin was diagnosed as having a condition called attention deficit disorder (ADD). Kevin had been considered hyperactive as a child and had great difficulty keeping up with his schoolwork. He was highly intelligent, with a genius-level IQ, but he had always had problems staying organized, paying attention, and controlling his temper and emotions.

ADD, which acts as a learning disability, is most common among children. About 3 to 5 percent of children under 18 have this condition, which stems from a biochemical dysfunction in the brain. Specialists now believe that at least 2 million adults continue to have ADD.[2]

ADD children usually grow up being told they are lazy, selfish, immature, and irresponsible. They often repeat patterns of failure throughout their childhood and adult lives. If Sheila had handled Kevin in the traditional manner, she may have had to fire a valuable and talented employee. But she recognized that Kevin's talent and personality were worth the extra effort. She knew he was a good person, that he was not irresponsible or selfish.

Kevin received medication to help control the ADD and learned how to control his emotionalism. His ability to concentrate and organize improved. But most important, Kevin's genius as an attorney blossomed and, as a result, so did his self-esteem. He has since won several cases for the firm and has helped to land some prestigious clients.

The "moral" of this story is that a problem employee may actually be turned into an opportunity. But this can only happen if managers and supervisors are willing to look beyond the standards and norms that are applied to most people. Sheila had never heard of ADD and had no idea what could be Kevin's problem, but she was not willing to give up on this valued employee who happened to be an occasional pain in the neck.

Learning Disabilities

Learning disabilities, such as attention deficit disorder and dyslexia (which causes the transposition of words and letters and makes reading difficult even for highly intelligent people like Albert Einstein), may exist in as much as 7 percent of the population. People often do not know they have these problems, or if they do, they have never been properly counseled as to how to cope with them. Of course, not every problem employee has a learning disability, but that is one possibility you may consider if you are working with someone who seems to be a responsible, capable, even talented individual, but is displaying inexplicable behavioral or competency problems.

The purpose of this chapter is to explore several areas that are potential causes for problem employees, including simple discipline problems. The most important message underlying all of these problems is that employers do not have the luxury these days of being able to replace their underproductive and unpotentialized employees. The discussion of the costs to productivity in the previous chapter bear this out. Effort must be directed toward your present employees to maximize their productivity. Both you and your employees can work together as a team to potentialize self-esteem in yourselves and directly impact your bottom line.

Although no employer can be expected to diagnose a troubled employee's problems, encouraging such an employee to seek professional help and giving assurance that it will not reflect on his job status, can be a step toward turning a problem into an opportunity for both of you.

Depression

Jana had worked at a medium-sized direct mail company for about three years. She was a database manager for some large national clients. She had always been an excellent worker, but her boss, Michael, began to notice that Jana seemed bored and uninterested in the work she used to love. She forgot things that had been clearly spelled out in meetings, turned in reports that lacked in detail, and often left the office at five o'clock sharp or even a few minutes earlier. In meetings with Michael and other workers she was unusually quiet and contributed little to brainstorming sessions. When questioned about ideas or plans for her clients, Jana responded with skepticism. She seemed to feel that it was not worth the effort to come up with any new plans or ideas.

One day, Michael asked Jana to come into his office. He told her, "You seem like the most unhappy person on the earth. Life is too short for this. I want to find out what's wrong and how I can help you."

Jana was stunned, thinking she had kept her feelings hidden. But she responded to Michael's sincere desire to help her. She began to tell him about some personal problems she was experiencing and said she had been considering seeing a psychologist for depression. Her hesitancy was due to a belief that people, including her bosses, would think she was mentally ill and may want to get rid of her.

Michael assured her that he supported her desire for counseling and wholeheartedly encouraged her to see a psychologist. He also promised total confidentiality about her problems to their superiors and offered to help her in any way at work that the counselor might suggest. His support and encouragement allowed Jana to get the help she needed and get back on track as a valued employee.

Unfortunately, many people have incorrect ideas about depression. As discussed in chapter 12, depression that lasts more than a couple of

weeks is considered clinical depression with a biochemical component. As many as 15 million Americans suffer from clinical depression
and many do not know it. Because society treats it with such prejudice,
people are often afraid to seek professional help for fear of being
tagged mentally ill or emotionally unstable.

Remember that clinical depression is serious, but it is also easily
treatable. Encouragement and support are necessary for an employee
who is going through depression. Acceptance of the situation and the
need for treatment will help return a good employee to his or her best.
If your company does not offer some type of assistance or counseling
program, find out what is available. At the very least, your health
insurance should cover some type of mental health treatment. If not,
discuss the need with those who make such decisions.

Drugs and Alcohol

Problems with drug and alcohol abuse is another critical area that
can sabotage a good employee. It is also an area that can be effectively
treated. The key, of course, is that the employee must want to be
treated. If the employee is not willing to get help or even to acknowledge the problem, there is little you can do as a supervisor. Some
companies are even making it policy to terminate an employee who
refuses treatment.

Assuming the employee is willing to undergo treatment, your role
is to provide encouragement and support. If the person is not able to
perform his or her job during treatment, a leave of absence may be in
order. Often, however, an employee who is working hard at recovery
is able to perform the job. The difficulty arises when bosses or
coworkers do not offer acceptance and support. You may need to
counsel other employees about how to work with the recovering addict.

Another problem to watch for is the codependency of the addict's
coworkers. You must be careful not to allow them or yourself to
become enablers for the addict's addictive behavior. Make sure the
recovering addict understands that he must be responsible for his own
work and his own mistakes. He cannot expect others to clean up his
messes or cover up his mistakes. It's OK to offer some extra help once
in a while, but the addict must know that he cannot depend on others
to carry his weight.

Remember, firing an employee with addictive problems without the opportunity for treatment not only results in the loss of a valuable human resource but also violates the Americans with Disabilities Act of 1992.

Physical Disabilities

There is one group of people who actually do say, "Thank God it's Monday because work ... brings joy of being active, not bored ... the joy of paying taxes."[3] These are people who are physically disabled, or challenged, as many prefer to call it. The Americans with Disabilities Act was passed in 1992, requiring employers with 15 or more workers to make reasonable accommodations to hire qualified disabled persons. Have you had the opportunity to consider hiring a disabled worker? Have you examined your beliefs about how that would or would not benefit your company?

Pizza Hut employs about 3,000 disabled workers out of their total workforce of 68,000. They have found that turnover rates for disabled Pizza Hut employees are one-fifth that of normal turnover rates. DuPont has also done 30 years of studies that show that workers with disabilities rank equal to or better than non-disabled employees on key job performance measures.[4] Steve Zivolich of Integrated Resources, which manages Pizza Hut's program, says: "Most handicapped people have not had the opportunity to work before. They appreciate having a job, and that gets translated into greater loyalty to the organization."[5]

The Department of Labor and the Government Accounting Office has estimated that half of all workers with disabilities can be employed with changes that cost less than $50, 20 percent require accommodations that cost from $50 to $500, and another 20 percent need accommodations that cost from $500 to $1,000.[6] If you have had reservations about working with disabled employees, consider that the costs are minor compared to the benefits.

The Generation Gap

If you are an older supervisor with a younger employee, you may experience some exasperation with the differing values of your young worker. That is natural as each generation tends to have different goals and lifestyles. This is particularly apparent between the two generational groups known as the Baby Boomers (born 1946–1964) and the Baby Busters (born 1965–1972).

The twentysomething Baby Busters tend to be a much more cynical and ambitious group than the thirty- and fortysomething Boomers. They are distrustful of the more idealistic Boomers and want to see the results of their hard work quickly. They are not as willing to be patient in seeking advancement and career goals. Try to remember that your young employees need concrete rewards, though not necessarily monetary. They want to have definite paths laid out for achievement. They may be hard workers, but they may not share your sense of loyalty and dedication to a company or career field. If they see greener pastures, they will probably leave you, but you can benefit from their practical approach to work while you have them.

If you are a younger supervisor with an older worker, you may have an age-old (pardon the pun) problem. Older workers often resent being told what to do and how to do it by younger bosses who may not have half as much experience as they. A young boss who is sensitive to this natural tendency can usually overcome it by treating older workers with the respect they deserve for their experience and accomplishments. Rather than viewing them as outdated, you can find a wealth of insight in older workers who have "seen it all" and have been through many tough changes.

There is always the possibility with either younger or older workers that bitterness and resentment toward you may dominate the relationship. Try kindness and respect and the other techniques discussed in this book, but if the person refuses to respond, do not let it undermine your authority. You may need the assistance of someone from human resources, or the person may have to be transferred. As long as you do not let stereotypes and different values prejudice your treatment of the person, you have done your best.

The Personality Clash

If you find your problem with the employee is a difference in personalities, reread the chapters on personality types. Remember to analyze whether someone is being rebellious or just acting out the inclinations of a command-person. Does the employee seem to be too nitpicky, or is it the attention to detail that comes naturally to a detail-person? Perhaps you are exasperated about a lack of attention to detail, when you realize you are dealing with an outgoing, sociable people-person. Or maybe it bugs you that this person is so quiet and meek, but you also remember that this support-person never complains about doing extra work and always has a pleasant attitude.

The key to resolving personality clashes is to remember that what bothers you most in another person may just be the strength you lack and need the most. The next time that gregarious people-person gets on your nerves, try sending her out to charm your most frustrating client. You'll learn to appreciate her talent for schmoozing!

There's Always One Rotten Apple

No matter how many wonderful employees you are blessed with over time, there is bound to be one or two that are downright incorrigible. They are the discipline problems that refuse to respond to any amount of fair treatment, second chances, or even disciplinary actions.

Ellen was a recent college graduate seeking a job in a television station. She wanted to be a reporter and believed that her college journalism courses and internships had prepared her to start in the business. As a member of the Baby Buster generation, Ellen also wanted quick advancement and immediate rewards.

She found an opening in a small station for a secretary and took the job, hoping to move into a reporter position as soon as possible. Though Ellen was an excellent worker, her abrasive style and obvious contempt for the secretarial job became to be a problem for her boss and coworkers. Ellen was politely asked on several occasions to be more patient and courteous with clients and advertisers. But her frustration with the job grew, and she began to refuse even fifteen minutes of overtime to finish typing an important letter.

Her boss finally set up a meeting with her to discuss her situation. He assured her that he understood her desire to move into news reporting, but asked her to understand that he needed her in her current job. He also pointed out that her lack of dedication to her performance in this job may indicate she was not ready to take on more responsibility. Ellen's angry response was to quit, without even giving two weeks' notice. The station was left without a replacement, and a great deal of chaos ensued until she could be replaced.

Ellen then began a bout of job-hopping among small suburban newspapers and radio stations, eventually being fired from each for her unreliability and uncooperative attitude. She is a truly capable worker and may even be an excellent reporter someday. But at this stage of her life, she has obviously not developed sufficient maturity to deal with the demands of a job.

Handling the Problem Employee

When dealing with any kind of problem employee, Peter Wylie and Mardy Grothe identify four ineffective behaviors in their book *Problem Employees*. These are: overreacting, avoiding confrontation, complaining (to other coworkers) and lecturing. As the authors point out, overreacting to the problem person with an angry or emotional response has only temporary effects on the offending employee and will lower respect for you in the eyes of other employees. Lecturing the employee and complaining to others also serve to lower your credibility and likewise have little or no effect on the employee's behavior. Avoiding the problem obviously won't help change it and will only allow it to get worse. If termination becomes necessary, it will be easier when the employee has had advance warning.[7]

The most effective method is to schedule a meeting with the employee at a time when neither of you is angry or upset. Have a carefully laid plan of specific undesirable behavior or performance lacks. Explain the implications and consequences of these problems, and offer support, both instructional and emotional, to help the employee correct them.

Let the employee tell his side of the story, and use that information to help analyze the possibility of any hidden problems, such as those discussed earlier. Ask for feedback on your management style and techniques and how you can help with the problem. Assure the employee that he is valuable to the organization and your goal is to see him succeed, not to punish him. Work out an agreement on simple objectives for the employee that can be measured at a later date.

At the next meeting, if there are signs that the employee is at least trying to meet the objectives, you are on the road to a win-win situation. If it is fairly obvious that no effort has been made to meet them, you should probably begin probationary warnings, depending on your company's individual personnel policies. And be sure to spell out exactly what behavior or non-compliance will result in termination.

The Truth About Performance Evaluations

As many as 30 million white collar careers will either hit the fast track or derail this year as a result of one of the most dreaded work experiences: the performance review. Whether giving or getting reviews, both managers and staffers find the experience uncomfortable. Hard economic times make evaluations even more stressful as they may be viewed as harbingers of job loss.

Even if there were no formal performance evaluations, you would still find yourself appraising others and being appraised. It is human nature to judge, even if its only a thought such as: *She's so organized, I know I can always count on her,* or, *He certainly seems willing, but he doesn't follow through.*

As far back as the Bible, there is an assessment of performance in the parable of the talents. To the worker who dug a hole and hid the one talent entrusted to him, instead of investing it so that it would multiply, his boss said, "You wicked, lazy servant!"[1]

Performance appraisals have been and will continue to be a part of life. When you were a child, your parents and teachers evaluated your abilities, your looks, and your personality. The self-esteem chapters in this book remind us that an appraisal process helped to form your present self-image—whether it be good or bad.

If they were done well, performance reviews would not be such dreaded experiences. They should highlight accomplishments, identify areas of improvement, set goals for the future, and offer a way to overcome discrimination through visible proof of achievements. The most important thing for supervisors to remember is that performance reviews are not an opportunity to bludgeon employees for their inadequacies. They are not a time to take revenge for irritating behavior.

If reviews are used as punitive devices, they will not only be ineffective but may actually aggravate problem situations by fostering resentment.

Here are some of the potential problems related to performance evaluations.

- Even though it's human nature to judge, it is also human nature to resist being judged.
- It's difficult for supervisors to be frank in their criticism when they want their group to appear in the best light.
- Some supervisors are so uncomfortable giving criticism that they consider reviews a necessary evil.
- In some cases, the relationship between the supervisor and staffer is damaged by the evaluation.
- Management rarely gives priority to performance appraisals, often putting them off as long as possible.
- One research study disclosed that only 30 percent of 25,000 employees found their personal performance rating effective in giving them information about their own work.
- Another research effort found that 40 percent of employees surveyed never knew they'd been evaluated.

The performance review is actually an opportunity for both the reviewer and the reviewee to help each other. By working together as a team, they can find ways to enhance their abilities. The supervisor is in a position to encourage the employee, and in the process, he may even help himself. Again, the golden rule expresses it well: Help your workers do their jobs as you would want your workers to help you do your job (or run your business).

The key word is empowerment. It is a mutual effort. You each have a chance to communicate what works, what doesn't, and how to make it work better. It is up to the supervisor to set up a "review-friendly" environment in which the employee doesn't feel intimidated. Even if there are problems to be addressed, the employee must feel valued in order to overcome the natural resistance to being judged.

To empower an employee, reviewers need to evaluate themselves in relation to each employee. They must consider their attitude toward the employee, the employee's individual personality, work style, and values. They must consider their own personality, work style, values, and relationship with the employee. Care must be taken that an employee is not unfairly evaluated according to the personality and style of the supervisor, instead of that of the employee. In other words, a support-person should not be evaluated as a command-person, or a people-person as a detail-person. Evaluate the employee according to best of his or her abilities, not yours.

Empowerment also means that it is the supervisor's job to create an environment that makes people want to perform. It is up to the employee to communicate what is needed for such an environment and follow through with promised performance when that environment is provided. The performance appraisal then becomes a two-way street, allowing both parties to determine how well they have lived up to their bargain, or whether some aspect of it needs revision.

One of the most important things for both reviewer and reviewee to do prior to an evaluation is to prepare properly. The reviewer needs to know the reviewee's working abilities before the review process begins. The reviewee needs to do a self-evaluation, prioritizing strengths, listing plans for overcoming any weaknesses, and discussing future potential. Some companies allow the employee to fill out a blank copy of the review form for comparison with that of their supervisor.

Lorraine Burke, human resources manager at Arco Oil and Gas, suggests an on-going review process with periodic reviews leading up to an annual evaluation. She says, "A manager and a subordinate should have informal discussions throughout the year [to review] changes in expectations and business objectives."[2]

A recently retired manager of hospital employees in three states strongly recommends quarterly evaluations. He points out that this method helps the employee to strengthen his or her work habits. Waiting for the annual review can allow unproductive work habits to become ingrained. Quarterly reviews also eliminate the element of surprise if a negative evaluation must be given.

Another crucial element for both reviewer and reviewee is the ability to listen. Interruptions should be prevented so that both parties can concentrate on listening and understanding each other. If a statement is unclear, neither person should hesitate to ask for clarification. It is advisable to take notes so that specific points can be referred to later for further discussion or clarification. Open dialogue should be encouraged to make the process less judgmental and more of a team effort. The process is only effective when both reviewer and reviewee can respond appropriately to each other.

A Look at Various Appraisal Systems

Trait System: If your company has a form that asks you to rate employees on a scale (usually 1 to 5) according to such criteria as "works well with others" or "punctual", and so on, it is using a trait evaluation system which is the oldest form of performance evaluation. The trait system, however, does not consider the content of a job.

Psychologists Peter Wylie and Mardy Grothe criticize that type of appraisal saying, "They don't get at the heart of employee performance because they don't get down to specific behavior. After an appraisal where one of these forms is used, employees often end up feeling like school kids who've just received their report cards. If their marks are high, they feel pretty good. If they're marks aren't so hot, they feel bad."[3]

Behavior Anchored Rating Scales (BARS): This method is well-suited to evaluating large numbers of employees who do the same job, such as cashiers or bank tellers. Degrees of competence in observable job behaviors are measured. The benefit of BARS is that it reduces subjectivity and inconsistency, but the downside is that it focuses too much attention on what the employee does, not on the outcome.

Management by Objective (MBO): The employee states in advance what he or she expects to accomplish on the job in the coming six months or year. Supervisors help the employee set up a plan for improving performance and accomplishing their goals. This evaluation approach is based on outcome rather than behavior or traits. Accountability is more precise and goal oriented. A series of milestones may be determined for the employee to work toward in a given period of time. This is the most accepted system for judging managers.

Critical Incidents Log: In each employee's file, managers keep anecdotal information on accomplishments and other significant events. This is consistent with the current tendency toward less rigid kinds of evaluations and more open-ended methods of assessing workers.

Finding a "Perfect 10": This system employs a comparison guide to analyze performance. People are promoted not because they achieve specific objectives but rather because they achieve better than others.

A current approach to performance evaluations recruits staffers in the practice of assessing one another and measuring the supervisory process. It is hoped that this peer-to-peer rating and subordinate-boss approach will make for a less intimidating, more nurturing method.

Self-assessment is also encouraged more and more, with the desired end being one of more emphasis on personal growth. This type of evaluation provides a reliable indicator of where the worker is in his or her career comfort. Filling out an evaluation form prior to a review allows employees to develop an understanding of their own expectations, accomplishments, and future plans.

Examine your company's evaluation system. Does it fall into one of the above categories? How is it used? Who sees it? Does it determine bonuses, promotions, raises? How could it be better designed? How could it be used to help supervisors and subordinates do their jobs better?

Remember that even a good formal evaluation system may have holes in it. It may not compensate for personality conflicts, office politics, or prejudicial thinking. For example, researchers have found that male bosses are sometimes afraid to evaluate women as honestly as they evaluate men.

Despite such inadequacies, the bottom line for any performance evaluation form is that three basics must be covered: clarify job expectations, review accomplishments, and plan for future performance and development.

Clarifying of Expectations

The expectations of managers and staffers in the workplace bring the golden rule into focus once again: cooperation, respect, consideration, support, confidence, capability, responsibility, independence, and flexibility. If there is one word, or concept, that ties all of these expectations together it is *communication*. Along with procedural and organizational requirements, political sensitivities and job competence, communication is vital for effective performance on the job, as well as effective evaluations of that performance.

Most of the reasons employees fail to perform well on the job are related to communication. The following ten reasons may seem simplistic, yet they are the most common reasons for the lack of production, interest, or commitment to a job:

1. Employees don't know why they should do something.

2. They don't know when to begin and end.
3. They don't know what they're supposed to do.
4. They don't know how to do something.
5. They think they are already doing something.
6. They think your way will not work or their way is better.
7. Something else is more important.
8. They're not rewarded for doing something—or not punished for not doing it.
9. They're rewarded for not doing something—or are punished for doing it.
10. They think they can't do something.

Clarifying why the employee isn't meeting the expected standards should be a priority. Specifics need to be probed. To do this effectively, the supervisor must be non-intimidating, nurturing, and constructive with criticism. Subjective judgments on the part of both the supervisor and the employee should be avoided. Each individual must try to offer objective appraisals of his or her actions and expectations.

Marilyn Johnson, clinical manager in the counseling program at Pennsylvania Hospital, says, "What people feel most concerned about is when the expectations are not clear, when performance is evaluated very subjectively."[4]

Companies such as the Tasty Baking Company and the Abington Memorial Hospital use a numerical rating system and detailed job criteria to clarify expectations and reduce subjectivity in evaluations. That way, supervisors "don't have the liberty to like or dislike a person," according to William Mahoney, vice president for human resources for the baking company.[5] The Abington Memorial Hospital system asks department heads to minimize subjectivity by identifying the responsibilities of each job with specific, detailed criteria.[6]

Reviewing Accomplishments

What are the criteria for appraising job responsibilities? Criteria for the appraisal must be representative of the time frame being evaluated. They must include core responsibilities, minimum requirements for performing the job, and the goals and objectives of the job. The key is to be specific, detailed, and as objective as possible in describing fulfillment of these criteria.

If you are using a rating system, more than four rating categories are usually inaccurate and inconsistent. According to management guru Douglas McGregor, it is possible to discriminate fairly accurately between outstanding, satisfactory, and unsatisfactory performers, but any attempt to make finer discriminations is a delusion.

Most supervisors are stuck with an evaluation form that they have inherited from their company. It may be confusing with far too many categories, or not enough categories. It may dwell on evaluating personality traits rather than specific work behavior or on areas not related to the job. If that is the case, it will be beneficial for the supervisor and the employee each to write a detailed summary and attach them to the form. That allows both the supervisor and the employee to utilize their own standards in reviewing and evaluating accomplishments on the job.

Whether you are giving formal or informal feedback, it should be given in a timely fashion. Let the employee know precisely when something happens. Don't wait six months to zap him. It should also be specific and clear. Whether a compliment or correction, specifics cover the territory, whereas general statements only create a fog; for example, "The course you took in business writing really paid off. The report you turned in last week allowed me to sell our idea to the boss." It helps to be objective as well. Instead of saying the report was outstanding, let the employee know the work was effective and that it accomplished its goal.

Planning for Future Performance and Development

Once the cause of a performance problem is determined, the supervisor and employee should work together to solve it. A developmental attitude toward the employee who needs assistance usually pays off. If a lack of technical know-how is the issue, further training should be explored by both the supervisor and the employee. If a lack of skill or experience is the problem, and it is felt that the employee is in the right job, it is important to recognize his or her best abilities while offering assurance that the company is willing to invest further mentoring and career development. Expressing confidence through statements such as "I know you can do it!" will go a long way in nurturing a budding star employee.

Capable and ambitious Dan was stagnating in a job he hated. His manager, Bob, who was not comfortable with supervisory responsibilities, hated his job, too, thus passing his negativity on to his subordinates. Although he gave passing reviews to the employees under him, his department languished in ineffectiveness and low productivity.

Eventually, Bob was replaced by John. John picked up on Dan's potential despite his defensive attitude left over from Bob's unaffirming administration. John encouraged Dan to begin trying out some of his ideas and stretching his skills. The empowerment quickly proved Dan to be the most valuable employee in the department. John had let him out of the bottle by helping him to set and evaluate new goals.

Five years later, when John accepted an out-of-town position, Dan was promoted to supervisor. John says his is the kind of success story that makes every manager look good.

Helping employees plan their career development contributes to the success of the business and its future. Be it a small business or a large corporation, managers who assist in producing successful growth for employees affect the growth of the business as well. Challenging assignments and money-making ideas should be discussed at evaluation time. That is one of the most important parts of goal setting.

Office manager for a busy dermatologist, Miriam Adams, offers this observation about goal setting: "It does not matter that employees are unable to immediately reach a goal—my greatest satisfaction comes in watching them conquer and grow in their continuing effort to achieve that goal. Employees with no purposeful goal contribute little to office growth or meaning within their own lives. As long as they keep striving is the important part. From a management standpoint, if we can be patient while they are striving for this goal, we will all be winners."

Supervisors must ask themselves whether they encourage employees' viewpoints for both the company's progress and theirs. Employees will feel valued and search for ways to "win the prize" for themselves and the company. Upper management must consider the ongoing importance of training and development of supervisors and employees through in-house service or continuing education—and offer financial support for these endeavors. All this adds to affirming the individual with healthier self-esteem, greater motivation, and less need for handholding on the part of management.

The Interpersonal Touch

In each segment of an appraisal, especially when dealing with problematic situations, a supervisor's listening skills are her most vital tool. This is also true for the employee. Listening is the link to understanding. Even body language can create a positive or negative influence. Eye contact is essential. Silence and nodding the head can be powerful. Another easy stratagem is to lean forward when a person speaks to you. Doing so conveys the message that you are listening, interested and ready to respond.

Evaluations usually cover both the positive and the negative. To best appraise a situation, likes and dislikes, moods and problems should be put on hold. Spontaneity, especially with praise, gives immediate affirmation. Caution and careful consideration of correction help diffuse the emotional response. When giving correction, always ask for feedback from the employee. That allows for a repetition of the communication in his or her own words for clarification. It is further effective for the supervisor to summarize discussions for further clarification.

When Evaluations Don't Go Well

What if, after the review and subsequent discussions of strengths and weaknesses, the reviewer and reviewee reach an impasse where matters of improvement are needed? Such a situation cannot be left unresolved, so you may have to involve the human resource department. Rebuttals usually dissipate when a third party joins in the problem solving. It is important for both supervisor and staffer to document the steps taken in working toward the resolution.

The Truth Is . . .

The truth about performance evaluations is that they are valuable to the process of loving the job you hate. Whether you are management or staff, you need feedback to function effectively. Even upper-level executives need feedback. A study compiled by the University of Toledo and Pennsylvania State University reported that 71 percent of executives interviewed in major U.S. companies are frustrated by the lack of performance feedback. Eighty-one percent said they are more likely to receive criticism than positive feedback. [7]

Performance evaluations are a communication process that should serve as a motivating tool and enhance productivity. Unmotivated workers who feel that management does not care about their development and success spell low productivity and possible failure for a business. Therefore, it is vital that both reviewer and reviewee understand that the only way to measure productivity, morale, and growth on the job is through some type of concrete evaluation process.

Beneficial as the process is, human nature makes both parties uncomfortable with it. It is difficult to sit down with another person and tell him his weaknesses and what he must do to improve. It is also difficult to listen to someone telling you these things. We all have a resistance to being judged. Perhaps that resistance is what also makes supervisors uncomfortable in judging their subordinates. It is understandable. After all, the words you use and the criticism you offer will affect your employees significantly. How they feel about their jobs, and possibly even themselves, can be directly influenced by what you say and how you treat them. Are you aware of the power you have to help make your employees productive, satisfied workers for your company?

Consider your impact carefully. That is not to say you should walk on eggshells and be loathe to express criticism or correction. But it is crucial that you be aware of how you present this information. When your staff believes that you are committed to their development, success, and satisfaction on the job, they will find genuinely constructive criticism of value. Most important, always remember to criticize or correct the behavior or work, not the person or personality.

Of course, no matter how good a supervisor you try to be, there will always be factors outside of your control. If two or more supervisors are involved in the review process, your recommendations for advancement or increases may be limited or not accepted. Though you must support management, you can express confidence in employees' efforts and a genuine commitment to helping them achieve goals in the future. Your support, including objective and constructive performance evaluations, will do even more to motivate most employees than the hoped-for raises. As one of my colleagues has reminded me, "Although you do not walk on water, a supervisor certainly is expected to get wet trying every day."

The Art of Motivation

Sondra believes the most effective means of motivating her employees is to remind them regularly that they could stand to do much better on their jobs, that they have yet to meet her standards for excellence, and that a little anxiety about whether they will be around to pick up their next paycheck can't hurt. Her employees respond to her behavior by quickly burning out on the job, producing mediocre work, or simply quitting in frustration and fear.

Bonnie's idea of effective motivation is to remind her employees about past accomplishments, acknowledge present achievements, provide constructive feedback that will improve performance, and offer an appropriate mix of tangible and intangible rewards on a consistent basis. The results? Bonnie's employees are interested in their work, willing and able to meet their own and the company's goals, and remain with the company as dedicated, loyal workers.

Who, would you say, has mastered the art of motivation?

Basically, there are two motivators for human beings, and one or the other of these is behind every behavior known to man. They are fear and desire.

Fear, of course, is the negative motivator. It is the one that Sondra uses. When an employer activates an employee's fears, it results in the employee's avoidance of something he perceives as harmful or painful—in this case, the work he is supposed to do. Although fear can be a valid and necessary motivator (in avoiding poisonous snakes, for instance), an employer needs to look at how fear motivates destructive behavior in the work environment.

Desire, on the other hand, is a positive motivator used by managers like Bonnie that can lead to achievement, success, and happiness. Of course, it can have its consequences, too, if the desire is a wrong one, but you will find that desire is a much more effective motivator for almost any goal.

You have undoubtedly heard the expression "You will catch more flies with honey than you will with vinegar." That is good to remember the next time you want to motivate your employee to work toward a goal. Desiring the rewards of success is far more stimulating than fearing the consequences of failure. Numerous psychological studies prove that animals and people are motivated to better results by rewards than by fear of punishment. Both motivators work, but the positive motivation is more conducive to reaching a goal or learning a new behavior.

You will find that true for motivating yourself, and you will especially find it true as you seek to motivate others. It is vital that managers know that they can better motivate their employees to greater success and achievement with the promise of rewards than with the threat of punishment.

Three Methods of Motivation

Fear and desire are the two basic motivators. But there are three *methods* for motivating others, according to *Success* magazine's "Motivation Guide." They are motivation by force, by manipulation or by persuasion.[1]

In the case of motivation by *force*, there are two types: physical or psychic. Physical force is fairly self-explanatory, but psychic force usually involves the more subtle domination of a strong personality over a weaker one, such as a command-person's natural tendency to dominate a support-person. That isn't necessarily bad, because it is natural for the command-person to be dominant in a relationship with a support-person. Both are cut out to be comfortable in this design. But, of course, such a relationship can be abused and carried too far.

A problem occurs when the dominant personality seeks to control the weaker personality, without allowing him or her any autonomy or individuality because there is a difference between dominating someone and controlling him. While a support-person may be content to allow a command-person to make the decisions and be the leader, he will eventually rebel if that person seems to take control of his very life. At the very least, the support-person will be miserable. The

"Motivation Guide" discusses psychic motivation in the following passage:

> The use of psychic force . . . frequently occurs in the workplace as well. Existence in some corporations can, over a number of years, render an individual helpless. One can only pity those who hate the jobs they go to every day. They suffer being exploited and degraded by insensitive bosses wielding the big stick of psychic authority. They feel trapped and powerless and remain ignorant of their own abilities and potentials. They exist in a prison of low self-esteem, and their wardens are not keen about liberating them.[2]

Obviously, psychic force is not the most beneficial way to motivate, though unfortunately, it is a common one.

The next method is motivation by manipulation. Whether this method is beneficial or not depends on the motives of the motivator. Sales contests and incentive programs rely heavily on manipulative motivation. They seek to dangle the proverbial carrot on a stick in order to entice people to perform or increase sales. The method can be very effective and generally, the people are aware and willing to be manipulated to gain the desired reward. Of course, misleading and deceptive sales gimmicks, truth-twisting propaganda, and outright lying also fall into the category of manipulation.

Author Alan Loy McGinnis brings added clarity to the distinction between positive motivation and negative manipulation: "You are a manipulator when you try to persuade people to do something that is not in their best interests but is in yours. You are a motivator when you find goals that will be good for both sides, then weld together a high-achieving, high-morale partnership to achieve them."[3]

The third method of motivation is by persuasion. To persuade someone is to cause him to believe something by reasoning with him. In other words, you seek to change his way of thinking or influence his actions by appealing to his reason or emotions.

That sounds very nice, but like manipulation, persuasion can be used negatively or positively. Persuasion that appeals to emotions and thoughts of fear, doubt, envy, and insecurity may work, but it is not effective in the long run. You don't build loyal, supportive, encouraging relationships among employees and coworkers that way. Another type of persuasion, however, can make a difference. "Motivating by gentle persuasion is standing by as people emerge from their shells and then helping them discover how high they can fly! It is really quite easy. Give praise and encouragement. Be tolerant. Listen. Try to understand. Share yourself. Search out the good in others. Help them dream. Dismiss their blunders and mistakes. Be kind. Love."[4]

Another key to motivating says that, "To the degree you give others what they want, they will give you what you want. That is the key to persuading, leading, motivating, selling, supervising, influencing, guiding others—getting people to do things for you."[5]

For a leader whose goal is to "get people to do things," it is important to start with a positive self-image. After all, how can you bring out the best in others if you aren't motivated by the best in yourself? Joseph Jaworski, chairman of the American Leadership Forum, lists these ten qualities as being essential to a leader. Give yourself a brief evaluation as you review it.[6]

1. **Mastery of self.** He must be in control of his emotions and must be in top physical condition.
2. **Empathy.** He must understand people and their concerns.
3. **Wholeness of purpose.** He must know what results he wants and do what is possible to make them happen. He must be positive and proactive, not reactive.
4. **Self-confidence.** The leader must be able to act despite doubts.
5. **Authenticity and congruence.** What the leader says and what he does must match up, as words match music in a song, to give him credibility.
6. **Ability to communicate.** Communication is essential to motivate and build morale.
7. **Ability to mediate.** The leader combines activities and builds coalitions.
8. **Integrity.** He must have mature ethical values.
9. **Intelligence.** If he does not know a thing himself, the leader must know how to get information and use it.
10. **Energy.** He must have the drive and stamina to stay on top.

With those ten characteristics, you are fully capable of developing the skill to motivate others.

To assist you in the fine art of motivation, here are some guidelines to follow, captured by the acronym MOTIVATE:

Maximize employee potential
Offer opportunities for growth
Trust employees to do their jobs
Involve employees in company decisions
Value employee differences
Allow for mistakes
Throw away threats and punishments
Encourage through praise and rewards

Maximize Employee Potential, or Potentialize

When employees feel that their skills have not been "put on ice" but have been evaluated and applied in the most effective manner for the position they are in, they feel more secure about stretching themselves. By placing small challenges along the way as well, employers will inspire employees to discover and use their God-given abilities. On the same note, giving employees the tools to do their jobs (i.e., well-working computers, informational seminars, clerical assistance, and so on) will also help them reach their fullest potential for the required tasks.

Offer Opportunities for Growth

Employees need goals to grow. They should be participating actively in the goal-setting processes—both their own and the company's. Sit down with employees and pinpoint the company's goals (especially those that include them), then *listen carefully* as they outline the goals that they have set for themselves; after all, they know themselves better than anyone else does. The knowledge that they have your support to help them reach the goals they have set is a surefire motivator.

Trust Employees to Do Their Jobs

Hovering—it's death to motivation. Give employees the responsibility for doing their job—then leave them alone to do it! Motivation is highest in organizations that encourage openness and trust. Free employees to assume more responsible tasks and, many experts say, productivity will bloom. Once a task is delegated to an employee, and you have left him alone to do the job, he will feel valued and respected.

If you continue to check up on him, you are sending a clear message that he can't be trusted. Delegating with trust can be empowering—and a powerful motivator.

Involve Employees in Company Decisions

Not every company decision can, or even should, involve employees. But many can. An important research finding in motivational psychology is that people who have no control over their destiny become passive, and they view the control of their lives as external to themselves. Ultimately, that feeling of externality can result in learned helplessness.[7] By bringing employees into the decision loop, you not only tap into a valuable resource, you let them know you value their input. Making them aware of decisions that affect them is a way to contribute to their successful development.

Value Employee Differences

As we have seen throughout this book, different people have different needs based on their personality types, work styles, lifestyles, and more. Recognizing those differences is crucial to effectively motivating an employee. After all, what satisfies one person may not satisfy another.

The observant manager will determine what meets the needs of employee A and employee Z, then act accordingly. For instance, an employee who is a people-person should be given the opportunity to work with others. Command-person employees would most likely enjoy more task-oriented activities, and so on. By the same token, some people require closer supervision than others. In order to optimize performance and individual motivation, an evaluation of the supervisory needs of the employee can determine how much participation is required of you.

Allow for Mistakes

It's going to happen: a mistake will occur, or a level of performance will not be quite up to par. That requires the delicate art of constructive criticism. Proverbs 12:18 states, "Reckless words pierce like a sword, but the tongue of the wise brings healing."[8] In order not to inhibit motivation or growth, and to bring about improvement, wisdom is required when giving feedback. If the employee knows that you are giving feedback with the intention of helping him improve performance, he will not be as defensive. It is also important to remember that you are to focus on the behavior, not the person. If the value of the person is under attack, criticism becomes demoralizing.

You should criticize in private, limit the feedback to one problem, offer assistance, provide suggestions on how the employee might improve his performance at the task, and state your confidence in his ability to correct or change the situation as necessary. Remember, too, that knowing a person may make a mistake yet still be a valuable employee goes a long way toward positive motivation.

Throw Away Threats and Punishments

Threatening with pink slips is not the most positive way to motivate employees. In fact, threats and punishments create that negative motivator we discussed earlier: fear. Avoidance behavior can become the norm with this approach, and it also encourages unpredictable and imprecise behavior.

"When employees cannot meet expectations and begin to feel helpless, they soon lose motivation. Employees who burn out are in situations where they feel no matter what they do they won't succeed," says Beverly Potter, a management consultant in Berkeley, California.[9] Worry over losing their job because they don't measure up, ends up becoming a self-fulfilling prophecy for the threatened employee.

Encourage through Praise and Rewards

It can be something as simple as a note handwritten on your letterhead or a brief call during the day. Just try to avoid the "no news is good news" method of approving employee performance. Recognition for a job well-done is without doubt one of the most essential motivators around. People need to feel important, as if the job they do counts in the grand scheme of things. Keep in mind that "Pleasant words are a honeycomb, sweet to the soul and healing to the bones."[10]

Bonuses and other more tangible rewards also serve as powerful motivators. In fact, a growing number of businesses are offering workers extra financial rewards for meeting results-oriented goals.

Such programs are attractive "because they let companies reward workers for good performance without raising base pay."[11] Keep in mind, too, that rewards should always be deserved, or they lose their impact for reinforcement and motivation.

Other Ways to Boost Motivation

1. Make sure employees understand your expectations. Don't allow misunderstanding about what you expect from an employee and what the employee *thinks* you expect to cause confusion and frustration.

2. Remove barriers to achievement. A pebble in one person's road to progress may be a boulder in someone else's. Seek to recognize and remove any barriers that may be discouraging an employee in his attempts to do a better job.

3. Be a listening ear. When employees have a complaint, be there to hear it. Productivity is hindered when even minor problems surface, and they can become blown out of proportion. It also contributes to an employee's feelings of worth to find that his concerns are of some significance to you.

4. Note improvements, large and small. This is especially important if you assigned an employee to a new task. Consistent reinforcement is vital in order to encourage progress in the early stages of performance.

5. Inspire by example. Show your employees how motivated you are through your behavior and attitude. Needless to say, if they see you plodding through the halls with a frown at the world and a grumble on your lips, they may be motivated to model your performance of negativity.

Keeping the Motivator Motivated

How do you manage your own motivation? One suggestion is from Proverbs: "He who refreshes others will himself be refreshed."[12]

Giving praise, encouraging and motivating others will, in and of itself, provide you with motivation. There's nothing like the hum of productivity and the smiles of many satisfied employees to help you love the job you have.

But there are a few other suggestions that should help you stay fresh and motivated as well.

Set Your Own Goals

Where do you want to be on your job in the next few months? Years? Take time to jot down those goals in a small journal. Read them periodically to help keep you motivated and focused.

Stay Informed

A wealth of information is available through seminars, cassettes, books, and magazines. Keep on top of your field by grabbing a few moments at lunch to head to your local library and do a little research, or sign up for a class that is work related or one that allows you to explore a subject you have always been interested in.

Sweep Away Negative Cobwebs from Your Thoughts

Having hassles on the job, car troubles, the post-holiday blahs? Sometimes your mind can become cluttered with life's little annoyances that seep into the job before you know it and prohibit you from being the motivator you are. Clear your mind by quiet meditation in the powerful words of the Bible or other inspirational book, take time to help a community organization that needs volunteers, or simply enjoy a few strolls in a park for a mind-clearing energy boost.

Associate with Positive People

Stay motivated by other motivators! Let yourself be inspired by fellow successful managers. Share your concerns, stimulate your thinking, and allow others to help you enlarge your capacity to enjoy the work you do.

The Most Important Part of the Art of Motivation

Alan Loy McGinnis tells the story of waiting to speak at a sales conference where awards were being given to the outstanding salespeople. One woman, who had performed spectacularly that year and who had made an extraordinary amount of money, gave all the credit to her sales manager.

As she stood before a crowd of 3,000 people clutching the award for best producer of the year, she recalled the slump she had been in two years before. The future had looked so bleak that she was ready to resign and had even called her supervisors several times to quit.

But the manager kept persuading her that she had not tried long enough and that she would not have hired her if she had not had unusual potential. The saleswoman's voice cracked as she related the story. Then she made this insightful remark: "For all those months when I wanted to quit and didn't think I had any future, Joan believed in me more than I believed in myself. She wanted me to succeed even more than I did."[13]

Whatever else that woman remembers about her manager will not compare to the power of her manager's motivation. Although the saleswoman herself may have been lacking in the motivation of desire, the manager was not. She had enough desire for both of them—enough even to replace her employee's fears.

What are the important ingredients that give you mastery in the fine art of motivation? They are very simple: Dispel the fear. Increase the desire. And seek to bring out the best in the people you manage.

Conclusion

The Wheel of Life

The Wheel of Life: Balance in an Unbalanced World

19

What do you want out of life? How will loving your job benefit your emotional needs and help you achieve your goals? If you don't like your job, you already know that it has affected your emotions, your physical well-being, and your personal life. It has made you feel out of balance. People need to feel a sense of wholeness, to know that their lives have made a difference and have a purpose.

Benjamin Franklin was a statesman, an inventor, and a publisher. He wrote and planned the script for his life and he acted it out. His life was a work of art—and Franklin himself was the artist. In *The Autobiography of Benjamin Franklin*, Benjamin Franklin himself offers encouragement with these words:

> *I entered upon the execution of this plan for self-examination, and continued it with occasional intermissions for some time. I was surprised to find myself so much fuller of faults than I had imagined; but I had the satisfaction of seeing them diminish.*[1]

His life illustrates that there is more to life than simply reacting to it—that, in fact, one can take a hand in shaping or influencing the events.

As you read this final chapter, please pay attention to where you are in your life today and where you want to be tomorrow. The living of life is too complex a process to say that all, or even some of it can be ordered or planned. It is a matter of degree. But if you choose to have a balanced life, it will be one that is rich in variety and choice. Like Benjamin Franklin, you can write the script for your life and see the future unfold.

The Wheel of Life: How the Spokes Support the Rim

One year I got a new bicycle for Christmas. It was the prettiest bike anywhere. My friend Sandy and I went riding, and I felt proud to be on my new bike. The ride was so smooth. All of a sudden Sandy got too close and her pedal got stuck in my front wheel. Five spokes were torn out. After the accident the wheel gave the rider a rough ride.

That's the way the wheel of life is. If one of the spokes is weak or missing, the ride is much more difficult. It takes a conscious effort to devote equal time to each area of your life. If you are unable to devote equal time, your life gets out of balance, which can result in confusion and chaos.

Let's consider the six primary areas that influence our lives:

1. Personal

How do you really get to know yourself?

How much time alone do you spend with yourself everyday? Most people are so busy that they don't take time out for themselves. I often ask my students, "How did you end up in that job or that marriage?" and they reply, "I don't know—but 30 years later, here I am."

Have you ever had a problem and for the life of you, you couldn't come up with the answer? Finally, you went to sleep and at three o'clock in the morning you woke up with a solution. That's no accident. You got quiet and the answer emerged.

The first way to get in touch with that personal part of you is by listening to your still, small voice within. You might have to make an appointment with yourself, but go ahead, do it. If someone wants to steal that time, tell that person that you already have an appointment.

The second way to get in touch with that personal part of you is by keeping a journal. That is not to be confused with keeping a diary. A journal is a personal recording of your thoughts, feelings, ideas, and dreams, not just a recording of who and what you see each day. And, if you decide to keep a journal, it is important that you know what will be done with it in the event of your death. You might decide to leave it to someone in your will or have it destroyed. In either case, should you keep a journal, make sure you have a plan for its disposal.

Several years ago, my life took a turn for the worse when I lost four loved ones almost simultaneously. I had been teaching students the power of writing their feelings in a journal. Now I had unbearable grief and I didn't know what to do with it. I pulled out my pen and began to write. I wrote for hours and for days. I wrote until I was too tired to move my hand across the paper. Something miraculous and healing happened as I transferred the thoughts and feelings from my heart and mind to the yellow legal pad in front of me. I began to feel relief, and as the months passed, I could see how far I had come. I only had to look at the months before to see—in my own handwriting—what I had overcome. In his book *Illusions*, Richard Bach says, "Sometimes we teach best what we most need to learn."[2] I'm grateful that I was given the opportunity to learn what I had been teaching.

I cannot say enough about the healing attributes of keeping a journal. Somehow, I was able to transfer all those feelings of grief out of me and onto the paper. As Benjamin Franklin so adeptly put it, there is great satisfaction in self-examination, especially when one is able to overcome many of life's challenges.

The third way you get in touch with that personal part of you is by identifying what gives you joy and making time for it. For the next few moments, think of some of the things that bring you joy. What are ten things that you do for fun? Next to that list write down the last time you did those things. Now ask yourself whether or not you would have done those things ten years ago. You probably have something on your fun list that you can't remember the last time you did it. You may also still be doing the exact same things today that you did ten years ago. That's not all bad, but are you allowing new people, opportunities, and challenges into your life, or are you stuck in the same old pattern? Have you changed your appetites, and are you open to life's best?

To get in touch with your personal part of you, listen to your still, small voice within; keep a record of your feelings and thoughts in a journal; make time for fun in your life; and, fourth, take basic steps toward achieving your goals.

Goals are statements of faith. They motivate you to reach new levels of maturity in every area of your life. In several of the seminars that I teach, the students spend at least an hour writing out their spiritual, family, vocational, and social goals. Those goals must be measurable, realistic, and obtainable, and you should have checkpoints for measuring your progress. If you have ever been on a diet, you know that you have a desired target weight and that you get on the scale to measure your progress.

The first step in setting goals is to evaluate your present situation and to determine where you are at the moment. After you identify where you are now you can decide where you choose to go and how you choose to get there. It will give you a sense of direction and purpose. Try to reduce the goals you choose to work on to a vital few, because you will need the time, energy, or money to carry out the plan for achieving them. Goal setting is a continual process, and it calls for a strong sense of priority.

One of the assignments that my students complete is a "Who am I?" collage. They take a piece of poster board and glue pictures from old magazines depicting where they are now and where they want to be. It helps them narrow down their present life and future goals. As they look at the pictures and think about them, they visualize what their future will look like. Here are some steps to follow as you set goals.

- Decide what is really important to you. Eliminate irrelevant activities or half-hearted desires.
- Set priorities and write each item out in order of importance. Your most important goals are As and Bs. Cs carry a lower priority.
- Every day write down the tasks and activities that will help you achieve high-priority goals. Also include the desired date of the accomplishment of each goal.
- Do it now. Don't get caught in procrastination. The first step is always the hardest. Reread your list at least three times a day and take action.
- Develop your action plan. What is the first thing you will do toward accomplishing your goal? When will you begin?
- Be thankful that what you want is right around the corner. Visualize yourself as having already accomplished your goal. Allow your mind to work for you and continue to have faith and patience. It will happen.
- Avoid distractions. Say no to interruptions and requests which clearly have nothing to do with your goals.
- Act it out. When you want something, act as if you already have it or have accomplished it. That will help you stay on your path of success. When you think and act confidently,

you will begin to feel, then actually become confident and successful.

Remember that goal setting is critical for your personal and professional success but that it is done by imperfect people in an imperfect world. Your goals will help you potentialize to be more of who you already are. They will recharge your batteries and keep you interesting and interested in this complicated thing called life.

And last, can you remember a teacher who had a major influence on your life? If you want another way to get in touch with that personal part of you find a mentor. A mentor is a person whom you respect who will take the time to help you grow. I have had a series of mentors in my life. When I was in high school, I had a high school counselor who said I would never make it at a big college like Ohio State. Fortunately, I had a wonderful English teacher, Ron Price, who believed in me. I couldn't wait to go to his English class. Even students who hated English loved his classes.

I went on to Ohio State, was accepted into the honor's college, and graduated with a 4.0 and a master's degree. At Ohio State, I had another mentor. In order to complete my education, I had to take a speech class. Public speaking was one of my biggest nightmares. The number one fear of all, according to the *Book of Lists*, is public speaking.[3] Because of a caring professor who could sense my fear and empathize with it, I was able to overcome my speaking anxiety, and I now make my living as a professional speaker. I've often wondered what career choice I would have made without her positive influence.

Less than ten years after graduating from Ohio State, I had another mentor. I met him at a National Speaker's Association convention. I wonder if he knows today what an impact he had on my life. I followed him to Dallas, Texas, where I attended his "Born to Win" seminar. It was more than an educational experience; it was a life-changing event. I had a spiritual awakening and have never been the same since. I listened to his advice, as have thousands of other people across the country. Zig Ziglar has been a source of continual inspiration for me, and I will always be grateful for his encouraging words. Find a mentor, and after you've grown—be a mentor. When you give yourself away, you get back one thousand-fold.

2. Social

The social part of the wheel has to do with your social conscience. What are you willing to give back to society, expecting nothing in return? Are you associated with a cause or a group? Are you involved with your church or supporting a political candidate? Have you taken time out of your busy schedule to help someone less fortunate than you? It's easy to feel sorry for yourself in today's crazy world. There is never enough time and always too much to do. But one way to get off the subject of yourself is to find someone who is less fortunate than you are and help him. It could always be worse. Think of the man who has no shoes—then think of the man who has no feet. I lightheartedly tell my students that the title of my next book will be *The Splinter in My Toe*. Have you ever noticed that when you have a splinter in your toe you can't think about all the other things in your life that are going right? Concentrate on your blessings instead of your weaknesses, give yourself away, and enjoy the intangible fruits of loving your fellow man.

3. Physical

Emerson said that your health is your wealth. The next part of the wheel is your physical self. How healthy are you? When was the last time you had a checkup? One day you are on the top of the world, and in a moment your health can be stolen from you. But you can learn to be preventive. A routine checkup can spot high blood pressure that might lead to a stroke or detect cancer in the early stages, when it's most easily treated.

The body can take a lot of punishment and still keep functioning. People can get along fairly well without a gallbladder, spleen, appendix, and bladder. We can even dispense with one kidney, two quarts of blood, half a brain, and all our teeth and still live. And when we die, we don't die all at once. The brain survives ten minutes; eyes, thirty minutes; ears, one hour; blood molecules, eighteen hours; bones, three days; and skin, five days. Isn't the human being awesome?

In spite of the body's incredible ability to function despite our abuse of it, most health professionals believe that disease is indeed self-caused by a reckless lifestyle and a disturbed mental outlook. Jobs that place high demands on workers and give little autonomy or appreciation are the biggest stress producers at work, resulting in negativity and physical challenges.

How Do You Stay Healthy?

You need to enjoy your work and have personal growth, intimate relationships, rest, exercise, and play. You need to pay attention to what you eat and laugh a lot. Laughing leads to greater respiratory activity, cardiovascular stimulation, and increased endorphin production. An English neurologist, writing in the *British Medical Journal,* deduced that if facial movements affect cranial blood flow, altering the brain temperature, many human mannerisms become biologically understandable. Smiling may be one way your body lets you feel better.

I remember walking into our neighborhood market some time ago. I enjoy wandering around the store and listening to the classical music. I ended up at the cookie counter where I ran into Walter, an older gentleman whom I'd known since childhood. He gave me a wink and a smile and asked if I ever got depressed. He said he never knew a girl who smiled so much. I told him that even if I get depressed, I still try to have a smile on my face. And usually the smile helps me get out of my mood. So smile a lot! You'll have a wonderful feeling of well-being. Laughter will help preserve your mental and physical health and prevent you from taking life too seriously.

What Is a Healthy Person?

There are some basic ingredients to being healthy:

- Healthy people are flexible. They are able to tolerate frustration and uncertainty.
- They are not defensive about the past, overwhelmed by the present, or fearful of the future.
- They are open-minded and nonjudgmental.
- They are willing to learn from others, but they can see merit in challenging traditional ways of doing things.
- They are able to make decisions without being influenced by others.
- They are sensitive and empathetic. They strive to be aware of other people's thoughts, feelings, and needs.

- They take care of their body because they understand that
  their physical health affects every area of their life. They
  listen to what their body is telling them. Illness and disease
  can be a message to take a new road in your life.

Your health is the most valuable possession you have. Our country
has laws that protect it. It cannot be bought or sold. Billions of dollars
are spent to keep it, improve it, and find it when it's lost. Some people
are enriched because of good health and others impoverished by bad
health. It is our well-being, our essence. Remember to treat your
physical well-being with respect. It deserves it!

4. Emotional

The emotional part of the wheel has to do with your relationship to
your family, friends, colleagues, and self. According to Pat Robertson,
parents don't spend enough time with their children. On the average,
among working parents, the father spends 37 seconds a day with his
children, and the mother spends 40 minutes. That is a sad commentary
on family togetherness in the nineties. It seems ironic that parenthood
remains the single greatest source of happiness for American men and
women, yet a minimal amount of time is spent in parenting.

To further complicate matters, women's roles have dramatically
changed in the last two decades. Women used to define themselves as
wives, mothers, and family nurturers. Now there are countless options
and opportunities for women, but the downside to these sweeping
changes is increased psychological and physical stress.

How do you keep your priorities in order? Do what you can to build
your self-esteem. Pay attention to what you are doing with your life,
and remember how valuable your relationships are. According to *New
Woman* magazine, more men than women have high self-esteem.[4] It
doesn't matter whether you are single or married, how old you are, or
whether or not you have children. American women still have a long
way to go when it comes to their self-esteem. Men are taught to "go
for it" from the time they play their first sport. Women are taught to
be humble and not to brag.

Take a few moments and answer the following questions:

1. List the ten most important people in your life.

2. When was the last time you told them how valuable they are to you?
3. When was the last time you looked in the mirror and said, "Self, I love me," "I am unique," or, "I'm special"?

I gave a seminar in Ohio to a group of insurance executives.

There were mostly men in the audience that day. I asked the audience those same questions. When I stepped down from the podium, the president of the association took the microphone and began to talk to his colleagues. He told them that several years earlier he had tried to tell his parents how he felt about them. His mother felt awkward and said, "John, you don't need to get into that with us—we know how you feel." And John said, "No, Mom, in 45 years, I can't remember ever telling you and Pop that I love you." He looked at the audience with tears in his eyes and said that not long after that he received a phone call. A drunken driver had gone across a double yellow line and killed his parents.

As I lecture around the country, I am constantly reminded of that story by the people that I meet. Don't wait until it is too late to say, "I love you."

5. Financial

This book is about life—and our careers are, or course, very much a part of our lives. After all, we spend our highest energy hours with people that most of us don't even choose to be with. Our families get what is left over after we've given the best of ourselves away during the day. Your job is necessary to support the other areas of your life, and that is probably why the financial part of the "wheel of life" has become too large and out of balance.

In some cases, we have little control over the hours we must work. If that is the case, you especially need to plan your activities with the wheel of life in mind. Concentrate on the areas of your life where you do have some control. Remember that your job is important, but it is not everything. Don't let your job rob you from knowing your spouse and children, from living a long, healthy life, or from developing an intimate relationship with God.

When looking at the financial part of your wheel, ask yourself, *What do I want out of life?* How will loving your job benefit your emotional needs and help you achieve your goals? Remember the Gallup poll referred to in the first chapter. It stated that 78 percent of people want interesting work.[5] That need placed second only to the desire for good health insurance and benefits. Other surveys have shown that a sense of purpose and a feeling of belonging, recognition, and appreciation are also important in a job. Though these were job-related surveys, the points relate to basic, fundamental human psychological needs. Everyone needs a sense of purpose, a feeling of belonging and appreciation.

Ask yourself these questions:

1. Does your job give you a sense of purpose?
2. Do you feel like you're accomplishing something in your life?
3. Do you feel you have an effect on the world?
4. Does your job give you a sense of belonging?
5. Does your job give you the opportunity to be recognized and appreciated for who you are and the talents you possess?

If you are trying to sell yourself on your current job, you need to decide how you will answer those questions. Your answers will have a tremendous impact on your personal motivation.

You can be motivated, fulfilled, successful, and profitable in your job. Don't give up on yourself or on your job yet. Believe that the possibilities are there, and you can even affect the bottom line in a positive way.

6. Spiritual

In some of my leadership seminars, I have invited Dr. Rene Rust, an author and ex-Catholic nun, to define spirituality for the students. She defines spirituality as believing in something outside of yourself. Some people call that outside influence their higher power, or God.

If you want to grow in the spiritual area of your life, it is important to have fellowship with people of like values and to pray or meditate on a regular basis. It is hard to hear what God has to say if you don't take time to listen.

You are not traveling through life alone. I can remember when I thought I was alone and I had to handle everything by myself. What a burden! It is refreshing to know that God is there during those dark moments in our lives when we cannot see daylight. He is there in our sadness and our joy, and if we are living in obedience he will guard our every step.

Henry J. Taylor was a well-known newspaper columnist and the son of a coal miner who owned a small mine in the hills of southeastern Ohio. Like any small boy, he wanted to explore and see what the mine was like. His father decided to take him into the mine. They got into a simple, barrel type elevator and went down to the bottom of the shaft. When they reached the bottom, they were met by the foreman who asked, "Henry, were you frightened coming down?" The boy said, "Yes, a little, until my father put his arm around me."

His father put his arm around him again and said, "Son, there will be many times in your life that will be dark and fearful, and your father will not always be there to put his arm around you. Learn to snuggle up close to God and let him do that."[6]

When you have a relationship with God, you will not face the trials and tribulations of life alone. Sunshine lies ahead, beyond the darkness. But many people lack confidence in God. They stay depressed and uncertain. People who lack confidence in God are like people who will not drive a car up a hill because they cannot be sure there is a road beyond the top of the hill. They have no faith.

On his first voyage to the New World, Christopher Columbus sailed for sixty-nine days through unknown waters, with a rebellious crew, struggling against terrible storms. One day's entry on his ship's log bears these five words alone: "This day we sailed on." There was no land in sight, no identifiable latitude or longitude to record, no odometer to say how many miles he had come, and no map to tell him how far he had to go. Sometimes in life, you don't know where you are or where you're going, but you know you have to go on. Pull out a piece of paper and write, "This day I sailed on," or, "This day I kept on going."

A Final Word from Jane

I have covered a lot of territory in this book, and I don't pretend to have all the answers. But if you'll try to put some of these ideas into action, you will discover a definite change in your situation. *Power* is the extent to which you can link your capacity for action with your inner capacity for reflection. In other words, how much of your mental and emotional insight can you put into action? If you've learned anything from this book, will you act on it?

Here are some things to think about as you reflect on changing the way you feel about your job.

1. Do you look forward to starting your day?
2. When you are handed a challenging assignment, do you dive into it with confidence?
3. Do you speak up, set limits, and say no when necessary?
4. Do you readily admit your own mistakes?
5. Do you refuse to allow someone else's bad mood or difficult behavior to affect your feelings about your job?
6. Do you think for yourself in spite of your boss or coworkers?
7. Do you think it's safe to be honest in your working relationships?
8. Does hard work exhilarate you?
9. Is your job satisfaction measured in other than monetary terms?
10. Do you walk straight and look people in the eye?

When you can answer yes to those questions, you know you are in a job that you love. And loving your job starts with loving yourself. There is no one else in the world like you, because God made you 100 percent unique. Life is too short to spend it in a job you hate.

Put these ideas into action. I've done the research and spelled them out for you, but they are not new. They have been discovered by countless others who believed that loving their life's work was vital to their mental and physical well-being—and their purpose on this earth. My sincere hope is that you will experience the joy in your job and your life that you deserve. After all, you are important to me. You are *my* life's work—my students. Your success is my success.

Resources for Further Personality Analysis

Barksdale, L. S., *Building Self-Esteem, 2nd ed.*, The Barksdale Foundation, 1989.

Bramson, Robert M., *Coping with Difficult People*, Anchor Press/Doubleday, 1981.

Hallesby, O., *Temperament and the Christian Faith*, Augsburg Publishing House, 1962.

LaHaye, Tim, *Your Temperament: Discover Its Potential*, Tyndale House Publishers, 1984.

———. *Transformed Temperaments*, Tyndale House Publishers, 1971.

Littauer, Florence, *Your Personality Tree*, Word Books, 1986.

———. *Personality Puzzle: Piecing Together the Personalities in Your Workplace*, Fleming H. Revell Company, 1992.

Notes

Chapter 1: "Why Do You Hate Your Job? The Work Force in Transition"

1. Michael Prowse, "Is America in Decline?" *Harvard Business Review*, July-August 1992, 45.

2. John Naisbitt and Patricia Aburdene, *Megatrends 2000* (New York: Avon Books, 1990), 24.

3. Robert Half International Survey, quoted in Caroline Arthur, "Working Is Worse in Japan," *American Demographics*, May 1992, 16.

4. Robert Levine, "Why Isn't Japan Happy?" *American Demographics*, June 1992, 59.

5. *Sales & Marketing Management*, February 1993, 79.

6. Patricia Braus, "What Workers Want," *American Demographics*, August 1992, 34.

7. Ibid., 30.

Chapter 2: "The Work Force in Transition: Understanding Diversity"

1. David B. Wolfe, "Business's Mid-Life Crisis," *American Demographics*, September 1992, 40.

2. Based on 1990 census figures.

3. R. Roosevelt Thomas, Jr., *Beyond Race and Gender* (New York: Amacom, 1991), 102–108.

4. Ibid.

5. Ibid.

6. *Working Woman*.

7. Based on total household incomes of African Americans, Hispanics, and Asians in the United States.

8. Prowse, "Is America in Decline?," 45.

9. Thomas, *Beyond Race and Gender*, 46–47.

10. Ibid., 47–48.

11. Some of these questions are taken from a survey on ethnic experiences in *Ethnic Identity: The Transformation of White America*, by Richard D. Alba, (New Haven: Yale Univ. Press, 1990).

Chapter 3: "Self-Esteem: The Basic Requirement for Job Satisfaction"

1. Romans 12:3, J. B. PHILLIPS: THE NEW TESTAMENT IN MODERN ENGLISH, Revised Edition. Copyright © J.B. Phillips 1958, 1960, 1972. Used by permission of Macmillan Publishing Co., Inc.

2. Romans 12:3, HOLY BIBLE, NEW INTERNATIONAL VERSION.
3. Romans 12:3, *The Living Bible* (Wheaton, Illinois: Tyndale House Publishers, 1971), used by permission.

Chapter 4: "Self-Esteem: How to Love the Personality You Hate"
1. 1 Corinthians 12:20–25, J.B. PHILLIPS.

Chapter 5: "Self-Esteem: How to Repair the Damage and Potentialize"
1. Leviticus 19:18, THE NEW KING JAMES VERSION. Copyright © 1979, 1980, 1982, Thomas Nelson, Inc., Publishers.
2. Walter Trobisch, *Love Yourself* (Downers Grove: InterVarsity Press, 1976), 11.

Chapter 6: "Are You Sure You're In the Right Job?"
1. Diane Holloway and Nancy Bishop, *Before You Say, "I Quit,"* (New York: Collier Books, MacMillan, 1990), 32.

Chapter 7: "How to Love the Job You're In"
1. Proverbs 23:7, THE NEW KING JAMES VERSION.
2. 1 Corinthians 13:4–8, HOLY BIBLE, NEW INTERNATIONAL VERSION.

Chapter 9: "How to Love the Coworker You Hate"
1. *Boardroom Reports*, 15 October 1992, 13.
2. Tim Kimmel, *Little House on the Freeway* (Portland: Multnomah Press, 1987), 203.

Chapter 10: "How to Love the Company You Hate"
1. Alan M. Webber, "What's So New about the New Economy?" *Harvard Business Review*, January-February 1993, 28.
2. Robert M. Hochheiser, *If You Want Guarantees, Buy a Toaster* (New York: Avon Books, 1991), 129.
3. Anne Wilson Schaef and Diane Fassel, *The Addictive Organization* (San Francisco: Harper, 1988), 57.
4. Quoted in Raju Narisetti, "Employees Manage to Improve Company in Yellow Springs," *Dayton Daily News*, Sunday, 9 February 1992, 1F, 4F.
5. Quoted in Kerry Rottenberger, "It's the Principle of the Thing," *Sales & Marketing Management*, October 1991, 80.

Chapter 11: "The Stress Cycle: Physical Signs"
1. Sandra Lotz Fisher, "Stress, Part I: Warning Signs and Identifying Characteristics," *Sales & Marketing Management*, November 1992, 94.
2. Ibid., 93.

3. National Federation of Independent Business (NFIB) nationwide survey, 1992.
4. David Heilbroner, "Repetitive Stress Injury," *Working Woman*, February 1993, 61.
5. Ibid.

Chapter 12: "The Stress Cycle: Mental/Emotional Signs"
1. Levine, "Why Isn't Japan Happy?," 60.
2. Quoted in Patti Watts, "Are Your Employees Burnout-Proof?" *Personnel*, September 1990, 13.

Chapter 13: "Handling the Two Bad Words: *Anger* and *Criticism*"
1. Dr. Hendrie Weisinger, "Criticism, How to Take It, How to Give It," *Boardroom Reports*, 15 August 1990, 13.

Chapter 14: "Coping with a Job Loss"
1. Martin Edelston, "Secrets of Better Firing," *Boardroom Reports*, 15 March 1993, 8.
2. Ibid.
3. Ibid.
4. Ibid.
5. David R. Hampton et al., *Organizational Behavior and the Practice of Management*, 5th Ed., (Glenview: Scott, Foresman & Co., 1986), 39.
6. Kenneth B. Matheny, "How to Reduce Stress in Your Work Life," *Boardroom Reports*, 1 December 1992, 13.
7. Marilyn Moats Kennedy, "The New Costs of Getting Hired," *Glamour*, June 1992, 119.
8. Marilyn Moats Kennedy, "You Need a Job?," *Glamour*, May 1992, 137.

Chapter 15: "The High Cost of Low Self-Esteem"
1. Sandra Lotz Fisher, "Stress: A Prescription for Change," *Sales & Marketing Management*, January 1993, 32.
2. Stephen Franklin, "Caution Saps Recovery; Some Jobs Gone Forever," *Dayton Daily News Smart Money*, 15 March 1993, 6.
3. "Hey, I'm Terrific," *Newsweek*, 17 February 1992, 50.
4. United States Statistical Abstract 1992, 100.
5. Larry Lipman, "Rising Medical Costs Threaten Future, Clinton Says," *Dayton Daily News*, 7 March 1993, 2F.
6. Study by Commerce Clearing House, Inc. and Markowich Consulting Group.
7. Study by MEDSTAT Systems Inc.
8. Allen Thorn, "Deal Now or Pay Later," *Miami Valley Business News*, September 1992, 1.

9. Ibid.
10. Ibid.
11. Literacy Volunteers of America.
12. Olsten Temporary Services Survey of North American Businesses, "Skills for Success," 1992.
13. Webber, "What's So New?," 42.
14. "B.E. 100s Roundtable," *Black Enterprise*, June 1992, 268.
15. Heilbroner, "Repetitive Stress," 61.
16. Webber, "What's So New?," 24–27.
17. J. Patrick Wright, *On a Clear Day You Can See General Motors*, (New York: Avon Books, 1979), 189–194.
18. Ibid., 194.
19. Ibid., 263.
20. Mike Casey, "GM Workers Simplify Form for Efficiency," *Dayton Daily News*, 22 March 1992, 1F.
21. Ibid.
22. Webber, "What's So New?," 32.
23. Ibid., 42.
24. Ibid., 27.
25. John Cunniff, "What's It Like in Trenches?," *Dayton Daily News*, 10 January 1993.
26. Ibid.
27. Webber, "What's So New?," 41.

Chapter 16: "How to Love the Employee You Hate"
1. Quoted in *Boardroom Reports*, 15 August 1990, 15.
2. Frank Wolkenberg, "Out of a Darkness," *New York Times Magazine*, 11 October 1987.
3. Phil Cheevers quoted in "List Industry Executive Now 'Renting' the Capabilities of Handicapped," *The Friday Report*, 3 January 1992.
4. Judith Waldrop, "The Cost of Hiring the Disabled," *American Demographics*, March 1991, 12.
5. Ibid.
6. Ibid.
7. Peter Wylie and Mardy Grothe, *Problem Employees*, (Belmont: Pitman Learning, Inc., 1981), 16–26.

Chapter 17: "The Truth About Performance Evaluation"
1. Matthew 25:14–30, HOLY BIBLE, NEW INTERNATIONAL VERSION.
2. Constance M. Green, "How to Turn Your Staff into Star Performers," *Black Enterprise*, July 1991, 62.
3. Wylie and Grothe, *Problem Employees*, 221.

4. Maida Odom, "Companies Rethink Ways They Evaluate Job Performance," *Dayton Daily News*, 18 October 1992.

5. Ibid.

6. Ibid.

7. "Execs Lack Performance Feedback," *Greater Cincinnati Business Reporter*, 1993.

Chapter 18: "The Art of Motivation"

1. *Getting There: A Personal Achievement Guide to Motivation*, Produced by *Success* magazine, 12–13.

2. Ibid.

3. Alan Loy McGinnis, *Bringing Out the Best in People*, (Minneapolis: Augsburg Publishing House, 1985), 21.

4. *Getting There*, 16.

5. Ibid., 9.

6. Ibid., 14.

7. Watts, "Are Your Employees Burnout-Proof?," 12.

8. Proverbs 12:18, *The NIV Study Bible*, The Zondervan Corporation, 1985.

9. Watts, "Are Your Employees Burnout-Proof?," 12.

10. Proverbs 16:24, *The NIV Study Bible*.

11. "Bonuses Replacing Raises in Pay," *Dayton Daily News*, Sunday, 4 October 1992, 4F.

12. Proverbs 11:25, *The NIV Study Bible*.

13. McGinnis, Bringing Out the Best, 40.

Chapter 19: "The Wheel of Life: Balance in an Unbalanced World"

1. Benjamin Franklin, *The Autobiography of Benjamin Franklin*, (New York: Macmillan, 1962).

2. Richard Bach, *Illusions* (Delacorte Press, 1977), 48.

3. Amy Wallace, *Book of Lists* (New York: Bantam, 1985).

4. Carin Rubinstein and Stephanie von Hirschberg, "New Woman's Report on Self-Esteem," *New Woman*, October 1992, 58–66.

5. Braus, "What Workers Want," 34.

6. From a sermon by the Rev. Robert E. Behrens, First United Church of Christ, Troy, Ohio, 24 June 1981.

About the Author

Before owning her own business, Jane Boucher (BOO-SHAY) was a counselor in Sarasota, Florida, where she worked with chemically dependent young people. Jane has her BS and MA from Ohio State University and has done doctoral work at the University of South Florida. She has been an adjunct professor at the University of Dayton, Wright State University, and Sinclair Community College.

Today Jane owns Boucher Consultants, a nationally recognized firm specializing in organizational effectiveness, professional growth, and communications. She is a consultant, professional speaker, author of three books, and a weekly newspaper columnist. Her clients include small businesses to Fortune 500 companies. Jane's client list includes among others, GM, IBM, the U.S. Air Force, and *Inc. Magazine,* and she has shared the platform with Ross Perot and General Norman Schwarzkopf.

The National Speakers Association awarded the CSP designation to Jane. She is one of the few Certified Speaking Professionals in the United States. Jane knew she had finally "made it" as a professional speaker when she was asked to fill in for the late, great, Ohio State University football coach, Woody Hayes.